"Meltzer [is] one of today's premier writers of non-fiction for young people." —*Boston Sunday Globe*

"[*There Comes a Time*] will help young readers understand the origins of the civil rights movement and the struggle for racial equality that continues today." —*The New York Times*

"An informative and inspiring work." —*Chicago Tribune*

★ "Starting with slavery, Meltzer traces the unjust attitudes and deeds behind the suffering that a lack of civil rights has meant for far too many people. . . . There is much violence to be reported, and Meltzer neither whitewashes nor belabors it. In a relatively short book, he manages to clearly describe events and convey the passion that energized this nonviolent movement."
—*Kirkus Reviews,* starred review

"[An] impressive survey of the civil rights movement. Meltzer places a human face on the commitment and determination necessary to shift centuries of discrimination."
—*Publishers Weekly*

"Meltzer details centuries of African-American history with an immediacy that keeps readers turning the pages. . . . For today's students, some of the events that dramatically unfold will seem like fiction, but the lengthy bibliography attests to its accuracy. This is nonfiction at its best. Meltzer's perceptive account will cause readers to think critically about where we have been and where we are going as a nation. A must for all collections."
—*School Library Journal*

"A stirring call to action." —*Booklist*

THERE COMES A TIME

The Struggle for Civil Rights

MILTON MELTZER

LANDMARK BOOKS®

Random House ⌂ New York

www.randomhouse.com/kids

Library of Congress Cataloging-in-Publication Data
Meltzer, Milton.
There comes a time : the struggle for civil rights / by Milton Meltzer.
    p. cm. — (Landmark books)
Includes bibliographical references and index.
SUMMARY: Presents an overview of the events in African American history
that culminated in the United States during the 1950s and 1960s and
represented a striving for equal rights.
ISBN 0-375-80407-2 (trade) — ISBN 0-375-90407-7 (lib. bdg.) —
ISBN 0-375-80414-5 (pbk.)
1. Afro-Americans—Civil rights—History—20th century—Juvenile literature.
2. Civil rights movements—United States—History—20th century—
Juvenile literature. 3. Slavery—United States—History—Juvenile literature.
4. United States—Race relations—Juvenile literature.
[1. Afro-Americans—Civil rights. 2. Civil rights movements. 3. Race relations.
4. Slavery.] I. Title. E185.61.M53 2001
973'.0496073 21; aa05 01-04—dc00   99-89550

First paperback edition January 2002

Printed in the United States of America 10 9 8 7 6 5 4 3 2 1

RANDOM HOUSE and colophon and LANDMARK BOOKS and colophon are
registered trademarks of Random House, Inc.

Photo credits are found on page 187.

For Jane and
John Assimacopoulos

Contents

THERE COMES
A TIME

The Struggle for Civil Rights

Foreword

THIS IS THE STORY OF A MOVEMENT pioneered by black people, but which came to represent the common interests of all Americans, regardless of color. FREEDOM was blazoned on the banners of the American Revolution. Yet millions of blacks, for far too long, have had to struggle to be truly free. Their color prevented their freedom to vote, to take part in government, to acquire an education, to move about without restriction, to marry whom they chose, to live where they liked, even to eat where they wished.

Emancipation from slavery came out of the Civil War. But for nearly a century after, patterns of segregation characterized American race relations. Some accommodated to it; most, in fact. But there were always others who protested against it. They

Members of CORE (Congress of Racial Equality) and the NAACP (National Association for the Advancement of Colored People) join in 1960 to picket a department store in Petersburg, Virginia, because it refuses to serve African Americans at the lunch counter.

were the forerunners of the modern civil rights movement.

To win freedom for African Americans is not, and has never been, a narrow interest. It affects the social, the economic, the political health of all Americans. Nor is the problem of discrimination only a regional, a Southern, issue. As you will see, the American public gradually realized that there was segregation not only in the South, but in the North and the East and the West as well. The movement helped Americans and their government to recognize that prejudice, that racism, lies behind economic insecurity and infects politics.

Protest? It is an expression of the discontent of one group resisting what is seen as an abuse of power by some other group. It is also a way to tell the world about it.

Here is how it happened . . .

CHAPTER 1

"We Don't Serve Negroes"

IT BEGINS WITH JOSEPH MCNEILL.

He is a freshman at North Carolina Agricultural and Technical College in Greensboro.

In town that Sunday, January 31, 1960, he tries to get something to eat at the local bus terminal.

"We don't serve Negroes," he is told.

Back at the dormitory, he tells his roommate, Ezell Blair, Jr., about the incident. "Isn't it time we do something about this?" he said. "We sure talk a lot about discrimination. But where's the action?" They call in two of their buddies, Franklin McCain and David Richmond, and cook up a plan.

The next day, February 1, they walk into the local Woolworth's, buy some school supplies, and get receipts for them. Then they go over to the lunch counter, sit down, and ask the waitress for coffee and doughnuts.

As expected, she says, "I'm sorry, we don't serve you here." The students reply, "We beg to differ with you. We've in fact already been served," and show her the receipts. The waitress is dumbfounded; she doesn't know what to do. "We wonder," one of the students says, "why you'd invite us in to serve us at one counter and deny us service at another. Is this a private club?"

Just then a policeman comes in off the street. What's this, black guys sitting at the lunch counter? What's going on? He walks up to them, knocking his club in his palm, looking mean and upset and disgusted. What should he do? This is something new and strange—blacks asking to eat at a place they know damn well is for whites only. His face reddens. Should he pull out his gun? Swing his club?

Those four young guys are not out to start a war. They sit there, and sit there, and sit there. They don't move. Serve us, is the message their bodies give off, or you'll have to drag us off our seats . . .

Four teenagers, looking for justice more than anything else. And what they do this day will launch a wave of lunch counter sit-ins to challenge segregation all across the South.

Photographed as they are forced to leave Woolworth's by a side door are (left to right) David Richmond, Franklin McCain, Ezell Blair, Jr., and Joseph McNeill.

Years later, someone asked Franklin McCain how he felt at the end of that historic day:

If it's possible to know what it means to have your soul cleaned—I felt pretty clean at that time. I probably felt better on that day than I've ever felt in my life. Seems like a lot of feelings of guilt suddenly left me, and I felt as though I had gained my manhood, and not only gained it, but had developed quite a lot of respect for it. Not Franklin McCain only as an individual, but I felt as though the manhood of a number of other black persons had been restored and had gotten some respect from just that one day.

CHAPTER 2

They Came in Chains

"JUST THAT ONE DAY . . ."

But the freedom movement didn't start on that one day. No, that day was just another stage in the long, long struggle of African Americans for full citizenship, for equality, for justice, for their simple human rights— a struggle that goes back more than 300 years (and still hasn't ended). Back to the time when African men, women, and children were the victims of a forced mass migration from their homelands to a strange new world.

It was the largest migration in history. There have been many other mass movements of people from one place to another. But most of the time, those people *wished* to change their lives. They hoped to build a new life in a better place.

A Dutch warship in 1619 lands a cargo of Africans at the colony of Jamestown, Virginia, selling them to a local merchant. It was the small beginning of the rapidly growing institution of American slavery.

Not so for the migration of Africans to America. They were *forced* to leave their homeland. From the fifteenth century into the nineteenth century about twenty million people were captured, bought, or kidnapped in Africa by European, Arab, and American slave traders. The aim was profit: to sell the Africans for labor on the plantations and in the mines of the Americas.

Africans were no better fitted physically to do the

labor forced upon them in America than were whites. Nor were blacks better fitted psychologically to live in slavery. In their homelands, Africans were farmers and herdsmen, craftsmen skilled in pottery and weaving, woodcarving and ironworking. They were traders and hunters, musicians and dancers, poets and sculptors. Some were princes and warriors, rulers of kingdoms large and small. Their cultures were rich and varied, as different from one another as were the African peoples themselves. Their colors, their languages, their food, their clothing differed greatly from one another.

Nevertheless, to most white Americans, blackness is seen as the color of slavery. What should be remembered is that long before America was colonized, people of every color—white, black, brown, yellow, red—had been forced to submit to slavery. Every corner of the earth has known slavery. And every people on earth has been its victim. With the same variety of brains and emotions, the same range of ability and personality, blacks could find slavery no more a blessing than could whites.

Shiploads of slaves did not begin to arrive in the English colonies of North America until the last part of the seventeenth century. Then blacks began to pour into the Southern colonies. Climate and the soil's fertility had made possible large-scale commercial crop production: tobacco in Virginia and North Carolina and indigo and

A newspaper advertisement (probably of the 1780s) promoting the sale of slaves at Ashley Ferry, near Charleston, South Carolina. Henry Laurens, who was a partner in the firm signing the ad and got rich off the slave trade, was elected President of the Continental Congress during the American Revolution.

rice in South Carolina and Georgia. Slaves were forced to work from dawn to dark, day after day, year after year. Their hours often ran to sixteen or eighteen a day. They were treated like an "animal tool" to produce the highest profit—cheap, totally controlled, and bound for a lifetime. By the early eighteenth century—and for another 150 years—black slavery was the foundation upon which Southern planters and Northern merchants built their wealth.

Cotton did not become a major crop until the 1790s, when Eli Whitney invented the cotton gin to simplify the labor of separating the cotton from its seed. Within ten years, more than 20,000 blacks were brought into Georgia and South Carolina to work in the cotton fields. Whitney's gin made cotton big business, while riveting the chains of slavery tighter than ever about the ankles of black men and women.

When the Dutch began to colonize New Netherland in 1609 (renamed New York when the British took control), they too were handicapped by an acute shortage of labor. Soon slaves were brought to Manhattan Island to work on the farms, public projects, and forts. When the English took control from the Dutch in 1664, slavery in New York increased. After New York, New Jersey had the next largest slave population of the middle colonies. Next door in William Penn's colony, the black population grew slowly, partly because the Quakers objected to slavery on moral and ethical grounds and partly because white labor opposed competition.

North of the middle colonies, in New England,

black slaves were imported very early. The English settlers of that region were ready to accept slavery, as long as it did not threaten their own freedom. Massachusetts recognized slavery officially in 1641, even before Virginia.

But because conditions of soil and climate stood in the way of making profitable plantations, white Northerners turned to the sea to get rich. Many fortunes were built upon commerce, fishing, whaling, shipbuilding—and especially slave trading. Several of the leading American business families were founded upon the slave trade. They helped to supply blacks to the sugar colonies of the West Indies and met the rapidly rising demand for slave labor in the colonies of the South. By the eighteenth century, New England could boast that it controlled the bulk of the slave trade in the New World.

Then, in 1776, with slavery and the slave trade solidly implanted throughout the colonies, the delegates to the Continental Congress declared their independence from Britain, shouting out to the world that "ALL MEN ARE CREATED EQUAL."

WHAT THE AFRICANS BROUGHT

What did Africans contribute to America, besides their forced physical labor? Nathan Huggins, professor of Afro-American studies at Harvard University, wrote this:

The Africans had brought techniques for growing crops, raising livestock, building dwellings, preparing food, weaving baskets, working metals, carving boats, netting fish, and trapping animals. As they had retained old work skills, they would learn new ones. They continued to grow rice, indigo, watermelons, and cotton, but they learned how to handle crops, like sugar and corn, that were new both to them and the Europeans. Workers familiar with hoes, casting nets, and looms also adjusted to a variety of European tools that were put into their hands. The white man recognized and profited from their capacities, even as he denied their existence. The slave could plan, organize, and direct as well as the master, perhaps better. In that way the slave would be more valuable, more useful, but also more threatening, for as the slave came to understand how little stood between his master and himself, his imagination would certainly conspire to find ways to defy the market system.

CHAPTER 3

All Men Are Created Equal

LOOK AT THOSE WORDS: "All Men are created equal . . . endowed . . . with certain unalienable Rights," including those to "Life, Liberty, and the Pursuit of Happiness . . ." How could any man be a slave if all men are created equal? How deeply did the men who wrote and signed the Declaration of Independence believe what it said?

Slavery did trouble many who became leaders of the American Revolution. Thinking of slavery, Thomas Jefferson said, "I tremble for my country when I reflect that God is just, that His justice cannot sleep forever." Patrick Henry declared, "I will not, I cannot, justify it." And George Washington wrote, "I shall be happily mistaken if they [the slaves] are not found to be a very

George Washington on his Virginia plantation. At the time of the Revolution, he owned 135 slaves.

troublesome species of property ere many years have passed over our heads."

These men were slaveholders. Their plantation homes were built by slave labor, attended by slave labor, supported by slaves who raised their rice, indigo, sugar, tobacco, and cotton.

Jefferson wrote into his first rough draft of the Declaration a condemnation of the slave trade (not of slavery itself). But slavery was too profitable a business in the colonies, and this paragraph was not acceptable to the Southern delegation. It was omitted from the final version as adopted by the Continental Congress on July 4, 1776.

Jefferson was probably not thinking of blacks when he wrote "all Men are created equal," for later he argued that the black man was an inferior being—perhaps by nature rather than only by condition. He and the other slaveholders who uttered anti-slavery sentiments rarely did anything concrete against slavery. They all showed the common racist belief in the inferiority of blacks. They were not willing to give up their property or to lose political influence through active opposition to slavery.

So it must be said that the phrase "all Men are created equal" was interpreted in a limited way by the Founding Fathers. Remember that they were the colonial elite, and their goal was not social revolution. The common people and their radical spokesmen—men such as Thomas Paine and John Woolman—took the phrase more literally.

Even the powerless slaves spoke out, petitioning for the freedom they claimed was theirs by natural right. Their refusal to be enslaved began very early, when some revolted aboard ship, while others committed suicide by leaping into the sea. There were frequent efforts to rebel, under pain of mutilation or death, throughout the 200 years of enslavement in North America. Sometimes there were organized insurrections. More often, slaves ran away rather than submit.

Again and again, throughout the Revolutionary War and later, blacks called for the end of slavery. They reminded the two and a half million white Americans how strange it was to shout "Liberty or death!" while holding three-quarters of a million black Americans in bondage.

Although blacks were at first kept out of Washington's army, eventually, under pressure of losses, the colonies changed that policy. About 5,000 blacks, slave

An engraving depicts Peter Salem, a slave given his freedom when he enlisted in the American forces, shooting Major John Pitcairn, a British officer, during the Battle of Bunker Hill on June 17, 1775.

and free, served under Washington's command, most of them in the same fighting units with whites, in both the South and the North. Those who were free had gained that status by various means. Some were born free. Some had been freed by their masters. Some bought their freedom after acquiring savings by one means or another. And others ran away to freedom, finding refuge in nonslave territory. One-tenth of the million blacks in the United States in 1800 were free. It was only marginal freedom, hemmed in by whites who could easily claim a black was a slave. The law gave blacks poor chance to defend themselves.

And there were other hardships to be endured, besides the fear of being taken back into slavery at any moment. Northern and Southern states denied free blacks the right to vote, their children could not go to public schools, they were shut out of churches or put into separate pews. It was segregation based upon color.

The war ended in victory, with most of the slaves still not free. They wondered what their blood had won for their people. They had helped secure America's freedom, but not their own.

In the North, slavery began to fade because there was no strong demand for slave labor. The new constitutions in the Northern states contained provisions that eventually put an end to the slave system.

In the South, however, slavery was strengthened

when the federal Constitution was drafted in 1787. To please the delegates from the lower South, the Constitution permitted slavery to remain legal. A compromise was reached between Northern and Southern delegates that allowed the South to count three-fifths of its slaves as a basis for representation in Congress. The African slave trade was permitted to go on for another twenty years. And the states were required to return fugitive slaves to their owners.

Who were the fifty-five citizens meeting in Philadelphia to draw up that Constitution? Whom did they represent? Not black people, who at the time numbered about one-fifth of the population of the United States. Not women, who were about half the population. Not Indians, whose land the colonists had taken by force or fraud. And not the poor whites, who could not vote because they owned no property.

So the Constitution created by the upper-class fifty-five did not do away with slavery; it legalized it.

It should be noted that nowhere in the Constitution do the words "slave" or "slavery" appear. The harsh facts are hidden beneath unnamed categories of being, unnamed people. Thus, in no way were the Founding Fathers honest or direct about the peculiar nature of the labor system of their new nation.

With the new government in office, Congress

quickly began to help the rich slaveholders. It passed the Fugitive Slave Act of 1793 to enforce the provision in the Constitution that persons "held to Service or Labour in one State" who escaped to another "shall be delivered up" to the owner. When the United States bought Louisiana from France in 1803, the institution of slavery was still further extended and entrenched by the establishment of many great sugarcane and cotton plantations in that vast region. In 1807 Congress passed a law banning the importation of African slaves, but its enforcement was lax and violations were many. And the strong demand for still more slave labor led to the spread of slave smuggling.

The Fugitive Slave Act of 1793 was made still more harsh by a new law, the Fugitive Slave Bill. Adopted in Congress as part of the Compromise of 1850, the law laid a heavy fine on federal marshals who did not arrest on demand any alleged runaway and a similar fine plus six months in prison for anyone who helped a runaway by giving him or her shelter, food, or any assistance whatsoever.

The passage of that law brought anti-slavery feelings to a boil. In the face of great obstacles and at great risk, thousands of men and women, black and white, had long devoted their lives to the cause of emancipation. Their crusade to free the slaves had become a crucial issue in American life.

Federal marshals, carrying out the 1850 Fugitive Slave Law, hunt down a fugitive slave in the Northern home where he had sought safety.

As early as 1775, a group of Philadelphia Quakers organized the first American anti-slavery society. Five years after the American Revolution, a group of free blacks, led by Prince Hall, who had fought in Washington's army, petitioned the Massachusetts legislature against the African slave trade. And in 1797 fugitive slaves living in Philadelphia petitioned Congress to protect their freedom. (Congress rejected their petition.)

Free blacks from the early 1800s became more and more active in the anti-slavery movement. The words "liberty" and "freedom" rang in their ears; they wanted the guarantee of those rights not only for themselves but for the black millions still in bondage. They acted through preaching and praying, resolutions and petitions, delegations and meetings, and by the creation of their own press or the support of abolitionist papers edited by whites like William Lloyd Garrison of the *Liberator.*

At the passage of the Fugitive Slave Bill, despair and panic swept over the black population of the North. More than 50,000 fugitives had found shelter north of the Mason-Dixon line. Many had married free blacks. Now none—fugitive or legally free—felt safe.

Northern writers such as James Russell Lowell, John Greenleaf Whittier, Ralph Waldo Emerson, and Henry David Thoreau thundered denunciations of the law, while Southerners complained it wasn't being strongly enforced.

"Under this law," said Frederick Douglass, a fugitive slave, "the oaths of any two villains (the capturer and the claimant) are sufficient to confine a free man to slavery for life." Douglass, one of the most brilliant Americans of the nineteenth century, started life as a slave on a Maryland plantation. He never knew his father and saw his mother only a few times before her death. At the age of eight, he was sent to Baltimore to work, first as a servant and then as a shipyard laborer. Though slaves were forbidden education, the boy managed to learn to read and write. In 1838, at the age of twenty-one, he fled slavery. His growth was spectacular. As lecturer, editor, writer, and organizer, he earned the leadership of African Americans in their struggle to emancipate themselves.

The abolitionists, rapidly growing in number now, had the double task of rescuing slaves, first from slavery, then from Northern captors. There were many attempts at fugitive slave rescue, some successful, some not. This open disobedience to federal law and the widespread assistance to fugitive slaves widened the gulf between those who bought and sold human beings and those who opposed such traffic.

Then in 1857, from the U.S. Supreme Court, came a decision that demonstrated the racist view that African Americans should not be accorded equal rights with whites. It was a ruling on the case of Dred Scott. He was a slave whose master had taken him into Minnesota, free territory. The slave claimed he was free because of his temporary residence on free soil. Chief Justice Roger B. Taney announced that for the sake of the country's "peace and harmony," a settlement of the crucial issue of black-white relations was necessary.

Taney, speaking for the Court, ruled that from the founding of the country, Negroes had been "considered as a subordinate and inferior class of beings" who therefore "had no rights which the white man was bound to respect." He further declared that Negroes could not rightfully become citizens of the United States, since the words of the Declaration of Independence and the Constitution were never meant to include Negroes. The Court was placing African Americans in a "less than human status" and thus assuring them unequal justice.

Slaveholders and slave-catchers were jubilant. In the North and West, abolitionists held great mass meetings in furious protest. Many friends of freedom lost hope. But Frederick Douglass said, "The Supreme Court is not the only power in this world. . . . Judge Taney cannot bail out the ocean, annihilate the firm old earth, or pluck the silvery star of liberty from our Northern sky."

In October 1859 a white abolitionist named John Brown and a small band of twenty-one men, including five blacks (two

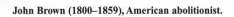

John Brown (1800–1859), American abolitionist.

of them runaway slaves), attempted to seize the federal arsenal at Harpers Ferry. His plan was to capture the arms and then liberate slaves everywhere by operating from strongholds in the mountains. But federal troops crushed the raiders. Ten of them were killed, five escaped, and the others were captured and hanged with their leader.

However rash John Brown's attempt was, his act dramatized the crisis over slavery. To the abolitionists, he became a great martyr. He had fired the first shots in the war that made compromise over slavery impossible. In March 1861 President Abraham Lincoln took office, pledged to end the extension of slavery into new territories. Six weeks later, the South fired on Fort Sumter and the Civil War began.

Many believed it a war to preserve the Union. But inevitably, it developed into a war to crush slavery.

HOLLOW MOCKERY

Annually, young America began celebrating the birth of its national independence with Fourth of July orators thundering tributes to the Founding Fathers and the Declaration of Independence. The ex-slave Frederick Douglass, noted orator and editor, was asked in 1852 to deliver the Fourth of July speech in Rochester, New York. He flung this challenge from African Americans:

*What to the American slave is your Fourth of
July? I answer, a day that reveals to him more
than all other days of the year, the gross
injustice and cruelty to which he is the constant
victim. To him your celebration is a sham; your
boasted liberty an unholy license; your national
greatness, swelling vanity; your sounds of
rejoicing are empty and heartless; your
denunciation of tyrants, brass-fronted
impudence; your shouts of liberty and equality
hollow mockery; your prayers and hymns,
your sermons and thanksgivings, with all your
religious parade and solemnity, are to him
mere bombast, fraud, deception, impiety, and
hypocrisy—a thin veil to cover up crimes which
would disgrace a nation of savages. There is
not a nation of the earth guilty of practices
more shocking and bloody than are the people
of these United States at this very hour. Go
where you may, search where you will, roam
through all the monarchies and despotisms of
the Old World, travel through South America,
search out every abuse and when you have
found the last, lay your facts by the side of
the everyday practices of this nation, and you*

will say with me that, for revolting barbarity and shameless hypocrisy, America reigns without a rival. . . .

Frederick Douglass (1817–1895), born a slave in Maryland, escaped to become a famous orator, writer, and editor, working ceaselessly to overthrow slavery and win equal rights for all African Americans.

CHAPTER 4

Liberation—and After?

IN 1861, AS THE CIVIL WAR BEGAN, blacks saw the possibility for great change in American race relations. There were four million slaves, a tiny black population in the free states, and a small number of free blacks in the South. As soon as Fort Sumter fell, black and white abolitionists tried to make Lincoln and the North realize that the Union cause would not triumph unless the war was fought to end slavery.

Victory could mean a change in the Constitution to recognize the principle of civil and political equality regardless of color. To advance that goal, Frederick Douglass insisted that both slaves and free blacks should be called into service to fight in an army of liberation.

Although Lincoln moved slowly, out of sensitivity to the loyalty of the border slave states that had stayed in the Union, he issued the Emancipation Proclamation on January 1, 1863. A military edict, it freed slaves only in those parts of the South still in rebellion. That meant millions of black people in the South and border states would remain enslaved until the final collapse of the Confederacy.

Lincoln's Proclamation was enough to convince blacks of the federal government's commitment to ending slavery. Even before then, thousands had begun to slip away from bondage and flee toward the Union armies. Lincoln opened the military to blacks in 1863. By the time the war ended, 180,000 black troops had served in the army and 30,000 in the navy. Ninety-three thousand came from the seceded states, 40,000 from the border states, and 52,000 from the free states. A quarter of a million had helped the military as laborers. To put an end to slavery, 38,000 African Americans gave their lives in battle.

When Lee's army surrendered in 1865, American slavery came to an end. In January 1866 the Thirteenth Amendment, abolishing slavery, became part of the Constitution.

Black soldiers did more than help win the war, crucial as that service was. They helped change the nation's treatment of blacks and blacks' conception of themselves.

Although they were not given equal treatment in promotion and, initially, in pay, it was in the army that many of the former slaves learned to read and write. For the first time in American history, they were treated equally before the law, at least in military courts. Their service had a profound impact upon them. From their ranks would come many of the black political leaders of the years to come.

The South at war's end was a shambles, its economy

Company E of the Fourth Colored Infantry, standing inspection outside their barracks at Fort Lincoln as the Civil War is nearing its end in 1865.

in ruins, many of its people killed or wounded. Desolation and starvation set in for both blacks and whites. To cope with urgent needs, Congress set up the Freedmen's Bureau. It helped blacks and poor whites find work and gain an education. Missionary and church groups sent in thousands of brave women, white and black, to open schools for the ex-slaves, young and old.

Emancipation meant that blacks were no longer officially "property." Newly set free, they hoped to begin a new life. But would they enjoy full citizenship and equality? Did emancipation imply any civil rights for the former slaves? Did freedom mean only the bare privilege of not being chained? If so, then it was a bitter mockery. The meaning of freedom itself would become fiercely debated and fought over for a long time to come.

The new president, Andrew Johnson, himself once a slaveholder, swiftly granted pardons to many Confederate leaders and made clear he would let their states back into the Union on easy terms. He withdrew all but a handful of federal troops from the South.

The white Southerners were determined to place rigid controls on the newly freed people. As their states formed new constitutions and began to elect officials, nowhere did they offer the ballot to blacks. Still clinging to the myth of white superiority, they held blacks were not fit to take part in politics and unable to learn how.

So only whites—the "superior" people—could vote in the fall elections of 1865. Prominent Confederates were placed in state and local office everywhere and the crucial task of Reconstruction placed in their hands. At once it was clear how they planned to carry it out. Black Codes, similar to slave codes, were adopted by the state legislatures, which in all but name restored the freed people to their old condition of slavery. "This is a white man's government," said the new governor of South Carolina, "and intended for white men only."

In Mississippi, the effect of the Black Code in Yazoo County was testified to by A. T. Morgan, a Union colonel who had made his home there. Under the code's provisions, he said, "Men and women were cheated, swindled, robbed, whipped, hunted with bloodhounds, shot, killed; nay, more, men were robbed of their wives, their children, their sweethearts, fathers, brothers, sons, saw their mothers, wives, sisters, seduced, betrayed, raped, and if Yazoo *law* afforded them any promise of redress, Yazoo *practice* gave them no remedy whatever."

In addition to Black Codes, whites conspired to use other means to keep blacks down. Five whites violently opposed to civil rights for blacks formed the Ku Klux Klan in 1865. The KKK spread with dizzying speed all over the country. By 1867 there were hundreds of local units operating in every state from Virginia to Texas. They formed an "Invisible Empire" commanded by Nathan Bedford Forrest, a former slave trader and Confederate general. The Klan was an underground terrorist army rebelling against the government. Its chief aim was to maintain or restore white supremacy by any means possible.

Three members of the Mississippi Ku Klux Klan in the disguises worn at the time of their capture.

The ex-slaves would not take such oppression lying down. In one state after another, they held rallies and conventions to protest racist laws and to demand that all political and legal barriers based upon color be torn down.

They wanted independence from white control, and autonomy both as individuals and as members of the community. They dressed as they liked, they left plantations when they chose, they quit churches controlled by whites and created their own, they strengthened the families they had reunited after slavery, they built up their own schools and benevolent societies.

And fundamental to everyday life, they demanded the right to control conditions under which they worked. Underpinning these hopes and aspirations was recognition of the fact that they could not have equal rights as citizens without the right to vote. The ballot was the emblem of citizenship. If you could vote, you could help shape the collective public life. So suffrage and equality before the law became the heart of black political action. Now the nation had the chance to live up to its republican creed. It was a goal that could only be achieved if the nation tore down all racial barriers and absorbed blacks fully into the civil and political order.

In Congress the Radical Republicans were a powerful force. The term "radical" in this usage meant something different from what it means now. It was applied chiefly to the position taken on slavery and the African Americans. Radical Republicans had been for the abolition of slavery and now demanded full citizenship for the freed people. Their leader in Congress was Thaddeus

Stevens, who fought for adoption of the Thirteenth, Fourteenth, and Fifteenth Amendments to the Constitution to guarantee full citizenship to the former slaves.

The Radical Republicans in Congress fought President Johnson's support of the Black Codes. They held hearings with scores of witnesses testifying to the horror of everyday life for the freed people. They concluded it was madness to place so much power in the hands of the Confederates. The Congress then passed bills—over Johnson's veto—for a sound Reconstruction program. Among them was the Civil Rights Act of 1866, guaranteeing the four million ex-slaves equality before the law. And to strengthen that guarantee of civil rights, the Fourteenth Amendment was adopted in 1868. It declared that blacks were citizens of the United States and entitled to equal treatment before the law.

In 1870 came the Fifteenth Amendment, which forbade interference with the core political right, the right to vote, on the basis of race, color, or previous condition of servitude. Along with the thirteenth, these constitutional amendments have provided the Congress with the authority to enact all the civil rights legislation that has become law since 1865. To get back into the Union, Southern states had to ratify the amendments.

Beginning in the fall of 1867, the Southern states, under the eye of the military, held the constitutional conventions that the Reconstruction Acts called for. A million blacks were now enfranchised, about the same number as whites. Despite centuries of oppression, black leaders arose to take seats in the constitutional conventions and the state legislatures, seats once reserved for whites only. Most of the new black leaders were self-educated, many of them preachers, some teachers, a few lawyers, the others farmers or artisans.

The new state lawmakers repealed the old slave codes and the Black Codes, as well as all other discriminatory laws regarding jury service, travel on railroads,

A woodcut showing the South Carolina legislature meeting in 1876, the last full year of Reconstruction.

steamboats, or stagecoaches, or seating in theaters. They started public school systems, which many states had never had, and found ways to raise the money to finance them. They made drastic reforms in the courts. Month after month, they studied, argued, debated, drafted bills, rewrote them, sought common interests, learned to strike compromises. They modernized old public buildings and constructed new ones. They set up state hospitals, opened new facilities for the blind, the deaf, the dumb, the insane. To protect workers' interests, they abolished all vagrancy laws, lowered tax rates on the tools and implements of mechanics and artisans. The rights of women were protected by laws that made employers pay married women's wages to them, instead of to their husbands. They encouraged the expansion of business and industry and raised money for the great program of Reconstruction on progressive principles of taxation.

Black Americans had at last found their place in government. It was the first time blacks shared in the public life of their town, county, state, and federal government. But never did they "rule" the South. At no time in Reconstruction did blacks control a state. Even though they were in a majority in Mississippi, Louisiana, and South Carolina, they did not dominate those governments.

During the Reconstruction years, fourteen blacks were elected to the U.S. House of Representatives and two to the U.S. Senate. Most of them had been state or local officials before coming to Congress and had parliamentary experience. Prejudiced historians, then and later, made unsubstantiated charges against the black legislators, blaming them for the ills that beset the Southern states. But more recent historical research has demonstrated what good things were done by the legislatures in which blacks served.

The new constitutional amendments entitled blacks to equal treatment before the law. But it soon became clear that few white Southerners paid any attention. To make sure blacks stayed in their place, many communities set aside "white" and "colored" seats in public places and on public transportation. Drinking fountains, waiting rooms, and even cemeteries were segregated in this way. This was the custom in many towns and cities across the nation, but in the South, it became law beginning in the 1870s. Jim Crow laws, they were called.

So in 1875 a new Civil Rights Act gave the citizens of every race and color the right to equal treatment in inns, public conveyances, theaters, and other places of public amusement. However, in the trading that took place to get needed votes, some of the bill's key provisions, including desegregation of the schools, were knocked out.

With only weak provisions for enforcement, the law remained largely a dead letter. And in 1883 the

A segregated drinking fountain somewhere in the South. African Americans were never allowed to forget their Jim Crow status for an instant.

Supreme Court ruled it unconstitutional.

Blacks emerging from slavery knew that the source of their old masters' power had been their ownership of the land. With slavery now dead, the freed people believed they had a right to a piece of the land they had made profitable for whites with their own sweat and blood. In the 1860s Congress gave away, through the Pacific Railway Acts, 100 million acres of public lands, lands that enriched the railroads and their investors. But they gave no land to the freed people. A proposal by the Radical Republicans to break up the Southern plantations and parcel them out to landless farmers, black and white, never became a reality.

So if black farmers wanted to live, they had to work

for others, under the rule of the planters, still lords of the manor. Instead of slave labor, there was now day labor, or tenant farming and sharecropping. Changes, yes, but it didn't feel much different from slavery. The people with land and money were still the people with power. And as the Reconstruction governments were forced out, the laws once again were being made by the planter and for the planter. And where the law did not do his will, the planter resorted to force to gain his ends.

The record of violence against blacks in the South during Reconstruction is one of the most brutal in our history. Whites who refused to respect the law organized masked racist gangs to make destructive assaults upon black rights, property, and lives, adding to the terror unleashed by the Ku Klux Klan.

The Republican Party, deserting Thaddeus Stevens's idealistic war aims of freeing and protecting the blacks, was now the party of the new industrialists and businessmen. The Democrats, the traditional party of the South and now dominated by former Confederates, found the Republican politicos ready to abandon blacks to their former masters. And eager to share in the economic future of the South.

When voting returns in the presidential election of 1876 became hotly disputed, the two parties made a deal. In return for giving the White House to the Republican candidate, Rutherford B. Hayes, federal troops were withdrawn from the South, big subsidies for important Southern improvements such as railroads were appropriated, and more federal jobs were filled by Southerners.

By 1878 this "compromise" had opened the way for the former Confederates to return to power in the South . . .

"JIM CROW"

"Jim Crow"—that term comes up again and again in this story. Its origin goes back to the day when, on a Cincinnati street in 1830, Thomas "Daddy" Rice, a famous white "blackface" minstrel, saw a ragged little black boy singing "Jump, Jim Crow." Rice copied the boy's lively song and dance and for years performed the act to great applause. Gradually, the words "Jim Crow" from this song came to be applied to the legal segregation of blacks from whites in everyday life.

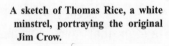

A sketch of Thomas Rice, a white minstrel, portraying the original Jim Crow.

CHAPTER 5

Separate—and Unequal

WITH THE FORMER CONFEDERATES again in the saddle, thousands of blacks in the South fled north or west. They were seeking ways to make a living without the slavelike conditions of the sharecropping system. The sharecropper made a contract to work on the planter's acres, usually in return for a third of the crop. But the sharecropper was often cheated out of his rightful portion, and protest was futile against the threat of whip or gun or jail.

They were seeking also to escape from the terrors of mobs by day and by night. Some settled on public lands opened to squatters by the government. Some went into the Native American territories. The largest number went to Kansas. But neither that state nor the federal government gave the new settlers any direct help.

Southerners, alarmed by the loss of both plantation hands and skilled artisans, tried persuasion and then force to keep blacks at home.

Yet the large majority of blacks did stay in the South. Only to suffer the most harrowing period of African American life since slavery itself. As Leon Litwack, a historian of that era, writes, whites "owned the land, the law, the police, the courts, the government, the armed forces, and the press." The political system "denied blacks a voice; the educational system denied them equal access and adequate resources; popular culture mocked their lives and aspirations; the economic system left them little room for ambition or hope; and the law and the courts functioned effectively at every level to protect, reinforce, and deepen their political powerlessness, economic dependence, and social segregation."

What way out might there be for blacks? An ex-slave, Booker T. Washington, head of the Tuskegee Institute in Alabama, a large and flourishing industrial school for blacks, offered an "uplift" program in a famous speech of 1895. He believed a policy of self-help and trade schools, as practiced in his own Tuskegee, would make blacks valuable to society and win its respect. Only then, he held, would the blessings of full citizenship be bestowed on them. His plan appealed to whites, both

Booker T. Washington, seated at the left front, with staff at the Tuskegee Institute in 1906.

North and South. It promised to provide a trained and docile labor supply, while it accepted an inferior position for blacks during the long years when they would be struggling to lift themselves up by their bootstraps.

Washington's speech was hailed nationally as the formula for peace between the races. Many whites believed it was the solution to the black problem. But John Hope, a young black educator, in 1896 challenged the Tuskegee head publicly. "If we are not striving for equality," he asked, "in heaven's name for what are we living? I want equality, nothing less. If equality, political, economic, and social, is the boon of other men in this great country of ours, then equality, political, economic, and social, is what we demand. . . ."

The Supreme Court did not see it that way. In 1883 the Court, made up mostly of Northerners and Republicans, had given approval to Jim Crow segregation of blacks in all states. Now, in 1896, in the *Plessy* v. *Ferguson* decision, the justices upheld the constitutionality of state laws providing "separate but equal" accommodations for blacks.

Justice John Harlan, in a strong dissent, wrote that "the judgment this day rendered will, in time, prove to be quite as pernicious as the decision made by this tribunal in the Dred Scott case. The thin disguise of equal accommodation . . . will not mislead anyone nor atone for the wrong this day done."

History proved him right. The *Plessy* decision greatly aided the spread of segregation on public transportation and in public places throughout the nation. Blacks justly contended that separate accommodations were rarely, if ever, equal.

By 1900 the myth of white supremacy gripped the national mind. The belief that the darker peoples were naturally inferior was spread everywhere by the press. Even the most respected newspapers and magazines were guilty of the crudest racism. The press played up crimes in which blacks were involved, creating the stereotype of the criminal black. Poems, stories, novels, cartoons, and jokes by the thousands sketched black people as dull, stupid, ignorant, vicious, and lazy. They were caricatured as clowns, thieves, liars.

The superiority of whites was universally preached. It became very easy for white Americans used to imposing their will on blacks to justify taking over Cuba, Puerto Rico, or the Philippines on the grounds that they were rescuing poor colored people from barbarism and offering them the blessings of civilization.

Around this time, blacks began to move from farm to city, in both the North and the South, seeking jobs and decent housing. They were packed into ghettoes that intensified all the ills of urban life. And wherever they went, Jim Crow, disfranchisement, and lynching followed.

As rights gained during Reconstruction were denied, blacks in the South who persisted in trying to vote were often beaten or killed. Small groups of white men hunted down and shot or hanged their African American victims, murders openly approved by their community. In

The lynching of two young black men—Abram Smith (left), 19, and Thomas Shipp, 18—in the public square of Marion, Indiana, in 1930. They were taken from the county jail where they had been held, charged with killing a white man and assaulting his girlfriend. The white crowd gathered under the tree seems to be enjoying the atrocity.

the decades following 1890, this kind of violence, called lynching, became a public spectacle. Grace Hale, who made a study of the culture of segregation in the South of 1890–1940, wrote:

It was a world where people who went to church some days watched or participated in the torture of their neighbors on others. . . . Lynchers drove cars, spectators used cameras, out-of-town visitors arrived on specially chartered excursion trains, and the towns and counties in which these horrifying events happened had newspapers, telegraph offices, and even radio stations that announced times and locations of these upcoming violent spectacles.

This deadly and often quiet form of vigilante "justice" had become a modern spectacle. It was like the ancient Romans flocking to the Coliseum in huge crowds to watch Christians being devoured by the lions. When eighteen-year-old Jesse Washington was the victim in a 1916 lynching in Waco, Texas, an estimated 15,000 white folks—men, women, and children—watched him mutilated and burned alive.

Spectacle lynchings were never the most common form of lynching. But they did occur again and again—in Kentucky, in Georgia, in Mississippi, in Arkansas, in South Carolina, in Maryland, in Florida. And in the North too—in Indiana and in Pennsylvania.

In 1900 the first bill designed to make lynching a federal offense was introduced by George H. White of North Carolina. (He was one of the six black congressmen

A crime conference held in Washington, D.C., is picketed by members of the NAACP, holding signs calling for passage of a Congressional bill to make lynching a federal crime.

to hold office briefly after Reconstruction ended.) The year before, 87 blacks and 12 white men had been lynched. During the decade from 1890 to 1900, 217 mob murders by hanging, burning, shooting, or beating were recorded. Newspapers from January to October, 1900, reported 114 lynchings, all but two in the South.

That year Frederick Douglass said, "Nor is the South alone responsible for this burning shame. . . . The sin against the Negro is both sectional and national; and until the voice of the North shall be heard in emphatic condemnation and withering reproach against these continued ruthless mob murders, it will remain equally involved with the South in this common crime."

In the ten years that followed, another 840 persons were lynched, and 304 more between 1920 and 1927. Of tens of thousands of lynchers and watchers, only 49 were indicted and only 4 sentenced to jail prior to 1930. The courts, police, and even the local clergy adopted an attitude of silent acquiescence. The records show that 5,165 Americans were lynched between 1882 and 1936.

What crime, if any, was committed by the victims of lynching? Ida B. Wells, black editor and the courageous pioneer of the anti-lynch campaign, studied the reports. Statistically, she proved that the "protection of white womanhood," as the South claimed, was not the basis for lynchings. In no given year had even half the blacks who were lynched been charged with rape or attempted rape. In 1900 less than 15 percent of those lynched had been so suspected. Lynching, she contended, was a form of intimidation to preserve the plantation economy and the white ballot box of the South.

CHAPTER 6

The Problem of the Twentieth Century

As THE 1900s BEGAN, W.E.B. Du Bois, an African American and one of America's most distinguished scholars, wrote that "the problem of the twentieth century is the problem of the color line." But was Booker T. Washington's solution to the problem the right one? Du Bois did not dispute the values of industrial education. "But," he said, "so far as Mr. Washington apologizes for injustice, North or South, [he] does not rightly value the privilege and duty of voting, belittles the emasculating effects of caste distinctions, and opposes the higher training and ambition of our brighter minds—so far as he, the South, or the Nation, does this—we must increasingly and firmly oppose them. By every civilized peaceful method we must strive for the rights which the world accords man."

In 1905 Du Bois and twenty-nine other black professionals met near Niagara Falls to issue a burning manifesto to the country based upon the principles of human brotherhood, freedom of speech and criticism, and exercise of all rights regardless of race. They would never stop protesting, they said, until America redressed its shameful treatment of black people.

W.E.B. Du Bois, scholar, author, editor, and unrelenting leader of the fight for civil rights.

The Niagara Movement led in 1910 to the organization of the National Association for the Advancement of Colored People (NAACP). The interracial NAACP declared its purposes were "to promote equality of rights and eradicate caste or race prejudice . . . to advance the interests of colored citizens; to secure for them impartial suffrage; and to increase their opportunities for securing justice in the courts, education for their children, employment according to their ability; and complete equality before the law."

The NAACP relied on legal actions in the courts as the chief means to those ends. Its first two important victories in the Supreme Court declared unconstitutional

The leaders of the Niagara Movement in 1905 in a photo taken on the Canadian side of the falls. Dr. Du Bois is second from the right in the second row.

the "grandfather clause" (limiting the right to vote) and city ordinances mandating residential segregation. But for a quarter of a century, litigation failed to destroy the structure of discrimination, diminish the prejudice blighting the nation, or hold back the increasing ghettoization of blacks. Southern states clung to their racial policies, and the national government did nothing to change that.

The mass migration of blacks to the cities and to the North continued. In the 1910s half a million blacks moved northward, with another 750,000 following in the 1920s. The North was anything but heaven. Blacks experienced segregation in the schools and neighborhoods, decaying housing milked by white slumlords, discrimination by employers and unions, brutality by the police.

In 1914 World War I broke out in Europe. American industries expanded to supply materials of war to the Allies opposing Germany. More and more blacks rushed north in the hope of finding work. Many got jobs better than anything they had known before. But their problems in crowded black ghettoes multiplied with their numbers. The government offered no protection against discrimination and segregation. In President Woodrow Wilson's 1912 campaign, he had promised "to see justice done to the colored people in every matter." But once in office, he put up Jim Crow barriers throughout the government.

In 1917 the United States entered the war, with Wilson proclaiming the nation was fighting "to make the world safe for democracy." But his world didn't seem to include black Americans. Segregation and discrimination

Arriving home at the end of World War I. These black troops of the 369th Infantry of the 93rd Division were in the trenches 191 days. They never lost a foot of ground and were the first unit of the Allies to reach the Rhine. They suffered casualties of 1,100 dead and wounded.

cut across all the armed services, in which 367,000 blacks served during the war. Nevertheless, blacks made a great record in combat, winning many citations for bravery. Maybe "democracy" would mean something when they got home?

It didn't. Once back home, the veterans quickly

learned nothing had changed. The wartime migration had much to do with racial turmoil. Whites had long been hostile to the attempts of blacks to lead a better life. During World War I, this hostility became even more heated when half a million Southern blacks moved up North. The new arrivals in the cities competed for jobs, housing, transportation, recreation, schooling, and political power. During the summer of 1919, civil disorders spread across the land, with lives lost in at least twenty-five of them, hundreds wounded, and homes burned down.

On June 1, 1921, in a thriving black neighborhood of Tulsa, Oklahoma, black families were burned alive in their homes or shot running away. The blacks shot back. The rioting whites killed from 200 to 300 black citizens, burned more than 1,000 homes, and razed one of the most prosperous business districts in the region. It was often prosperous blacks, few as they were, that whites targeted, regarding them as "uppity Negroes."

Yet though little else had changed, blacks were allowed to vote. The first black since Reconstruction was elected to Congress from Chicago in 1928. Local offices too were won by blacks in several cities. Grouped in the North in large enough numbers, black voters had to be taken into account when political parties competed for office.

If hope for a better life slowly rose out of this

change, it was strengthened spiritually by what became known as the Harlem Renaissance. Young African American artists and writers, centering in that part of New York City, entered one of their most productive periods. They celebrated their roots in Africa, attacked racial oppression, freed themselves from white symbols and images, and found their own unique ways to create art in many forms.

Langston Hughes (1902–1967), a leading figure in the Harlem Renaissance. After publication in 1926 of his first book, *The Weary Blues*, he was acclaimed the poet laureate of his people.

Their talents won the attention of white America and stimulated the pride of African Americans in their people and their traditions. Individually and in groups, blacks protested militantly against oppression and for civil rights. No longer could whites say that blacks were content with the way things were, that they didn't consider the rights and duties of citizenship important.

With the crash of the stock market in 1929, the Great Depression began. For most blacks, hard times were much like old times. As economic disaster became widespread, proportionately more blacks than whites lost their jobs. By 1931 one out of three black workers was unemployed. No one is starving, said President Herbert Hoover, business will be better soon. He was wrong; unemployment piled higher and higher until fifteen million were out of work. People lost jobs, homes, hope. Breadlines and soup kitchens were everywhere.

In 1933 a new president took office. Franklin D. Roosevelt faced the fact that "one third of a nation is ill-fed, ill-housed, ill-clothed." He launched many programs, which he called the New Deal, to help the millions of desperate Americans, black as well as white. His government agencies hired far more blacks than any Administration before him. Billions of dollars were provided for public works—new hospitals, community centers, libraries, schools, playgrounds—which blacks too shared.

A new labor law protected the right to organize for better wages and working conditions. Industrial unions sprang up, embracing millions of workers regardless of color. Many African Americans were elected to high posts in the mixed unions.

The New Deal projects did much to help blacks in those harsh times. But little to advance racial equality. When anti-lynching bills were filibustered to death in the Senate, FDR, claiming he needed Southern votes to pass other legislation, was silent. Unemployed blacks got lower relief benefits than whites. Some federal agencies discriminated against blacks in their hiring policies. The Social Security Act, adopted in 1935, provided for unemployment compensation and old-age insurance and pensions. But it excluded domestic and agricultural laborers, which cut off many working blacks from its benefits.

Still, the New Deal's real and symbolic aid to African Americans raised hope for more racial reforms. The First Lady, Eleanor Roosevelt, and other high-level government officials developed close ties with civil rights groups. The men FDR appointed to the Supreme Court wrote decisions in the 1930s that increasingly cut down racist practices. Progress, when it was made, happened in fits and starts. There was no steady march forward. The majority of whites, their minds and emotions crippled by ignorance, fear, and prejudice, remained opposed to desegregation and equal opportunities for blacks.

Meanwhile, across the Atlantic, in Germany, a dictatorship was beginning to demonstrate, with stunning cruelty, the effects of prejudice and racism.

CHAPTER 7

Without Fear, Without Compromise, Without Hatred

In the same year that Roosevelt entered the White House, Adolf Hitler became the dictator of Germany. His doctrine of racial superiority led at once to the oppression of minorities—political, ethnic, religious. "I have naturally the right to destroy millions of men of inferior races who increase like vermin," he said. His goal, he publicly announced, was "the annihilation of the Jewish race throughout Europe."

African Americans knew what that doctrine of racial supremacy meant. They did not have to wait for Hitler to murder millions to find out. But the democracies took no concerted action to halt Hitler's aggressive moves, and in 1939 he launched World War II. America began to prepare for what seemed inevitable involvement, building up a large fighting force and making the ships, tanks, planes, guns, and ammunition that would be needed.

The armed forces were segregated at that time, and discrimination was common. So too in the war industries. Blacks had great trouble getting jobs. Federal officials spoke out against Jim Crow, but industry paid no attention. Work for blacks pushing a broom? Cleaning a rest room? Okay. But not as airplane mechanics or ship welders.

Demands for equal rights and anti-discrimination planks in the party's platform are made by African Americans picketing outside the Democratic National Convention in Philadelphia in 1948.

What to do about it? On the other side of the world, in India, Mohandas K. Gandhi had been leading direct-action campaigns since the 1920s to break Great Britain's hold on his people. He called for a boycott on foreign goods, a refusal to attend governmental schools, and a refusal to pay taxes. All these activities were to be carried out without violence.

Gandhi's principle of peaceful, nonviolent resistance to oppression appealed to several African American leaders. When they saw that private pleas and petitions for equality got nowhere, they decided that powerful and peaceful mass action was needed. In January 1941 A. Philip Randolph, head of the Brotherhood of Sleeping Car Porters, proposed a march on Washington to demand that the government do something.

FDR was alarmed at signs of mass protest in a time of crisis. He tried to have the march called off, but the black leaders refused. Then Roosevelt said, no need to march; I'll do what you ask. And on June 25, 1941, he issued Executive Order 8802, banning discrimination in defense industries or in government "because of race, creed, color, or national origin." A Fair Employment Practices Commission (FEPC) was set up to carry out the order. For the first time since the Emancipation Proclamation, a president had issued an order protecting the rights of African Americans.

A great beginning. But only that. Much more had to be done. The need for continuous pressure was great.

In December 1941, following the attack on Pearl Harbor by Hitler's ally Japan, the United States entered the war. But did America's leaders see it as a war against racism? A war with a moral purpose? If it had, it would have done more to eliminate racial segregation. Yet Jim

African American women picket a Woolworth's store for its refusal to hire black saleswomen.

Crow continued to exist, North and South. And despite FDR's order, racial discrimination in employment continued, for the FEPC orders were not enforced.

In February 1942 all people of Japanese ancestry were taken from their homes and put in internment camps for the duration of the war. The government's assumption was that because we were at war with Japan, anyone of Japanese descent must be considered a potential traitor or enemy. By that reasoning, German Americans and Italian Americans too should have been treated in the same way. Clearly, it was because the Japanese were people of color that the government acted as it did. It was another blow against racial equality.

In the spring of 1942, racial tensions exploded in Detroit, a center for war industries where blacks and whites contended for jobs and housing. The riot ended only when 2,500 federal troops were sent in. Of the thirty-four people killed during those three days, twenty-four were black, seventeen of them shot by police.

In the South too, blacks resisted racial injustice during the war years. In the steel town of Fairfield, Alabama, twelve-year-old Jim McWilliams led a strike of black newsboys against the *Birmingham News* when it placed a heavy burden on them while letting the white kids off easy. After two weeks, the paper agreed to the black newsboys' terms.

There was no organization focused on civil rights using nonviolent action at that time. The NAACP usually relied on lawsuits and educational campaigns, not demonstrations. But the ground had been seeded by Randolph's action. Soon after, a biracial group in Chicago began to study Gandhi's nonviolent methods. They formed the Congress of Racial Equality (CORE) in 1942, dedicating themselves to confronting racial injustice "without fear, without compromise, and without hatred." CORE people were the first to try the sit-in method, again and again, at a small eating place in Chicago. Their group refused to leave until all of them were served. Soon management began serving all alike.

James Farmer, one of CORE's founders, traveled the country to spread the word, and CORE groups formed

James Farmer, one of the founders of CORE in Chicago in 1942. An advocate of nonviolent resistance, he led many actions during the civil rights movement.

in other cities. In 1943, sixty-five members sat in at Stoners, an expensive all-white restaurant in Chicago. It was a success, ending its segregationist policy. In New Jersey, in Detroit, in Cleveland, in Los Angeles—Northern places—CORE groups integrated amusement parks, theaters, swimming pools, public baths. Through such direct action and through summer workshops, CORE trained hundreds in the techniques of nonviolent action. They were lessons that would prove to be decisive in years to come.

NONVIOLENT RESISTANCE

The tradition of nonviolence is an old one in the United States. Men and women have resisted the call to violent action in various ways throughout history, from the colonial wars and the American Revolution down to the many conflicts that bled Americans in the twentieth century. They invented a hundred quiet or dramatic ways to protest war and uphold their conviction that peaceful solutions to conflicts between or within nations are possible. And when the government has not recognized their right to stand by their conscience, they have been jailed, flogged, deported, even murdered.

In the Second World War, for example, about 50,000 conscientious objectors accepted assignment to the armed forces, but did only noncombatant duty. Another 12,000 entered the civilian public service camps. And 6,000 absolutists went to prison rather than take part in any aspect of the war. They believed warfare was so evil, it had to be resisted.

Many peace-seekers hold to Gandhi's use of nonviolent resistance as a force for social change. The Indian leader advised building local committees grounded in truth, justice, poverty, and mutual aid. He encouraged the use of mass civil disobedience and noncooperation when the state interfered with constructive programs.

Gandhi's policy won independence for India without bringing about a bloody war between his people and the occupying British.

Nonviolent tactics against racial discrimination would be used more and more often as the struggle for civil rights in America intensified.

CHAPTER 8

The Court's *Brown* Decision

THE FIGHTING ENDED IN AUGUST 1945 with the defeat of Germany and Japan. The war changed America in several ways. For many of its 150 million citizens, the huge war production industries had meant more money in the pocket and more goods to spend it on. Yet what had this second "war to save the world for democracy" done for democracy at home?

If anything, the concept of racial supremacy had been pounded in even more heavily. The media had joined the military in instilling hatred. Racial prejudice had flared on the pages of the press. *Time* magazine called the Japanese troops "rodents" and asked for their extermination. Admiral William T. Halsey boasted in a newsreel that "we are drowning and burning the bestial apes all over the Pacific." The *New York Times* carried an ad featuring a Japanese face with the headline RAT POISON WANTED. The process of dehumanizing the enemy so you could more readily kill him was similar to Hitler's labeling the Jews "lice" and "vermin" as he sent them to the gas chamber.

Only six months after the war's ending, a mob attempted to lynch blacks in Columbia, Tennessee, a small town of 8,000 whites and 3,000 blacks. A white store owner had slapped the mother of a black Navy veteran, James Stephenson. Enraged, he'd punched the white man and knocked him through the store's window. News of the incident raced through town and

A racist propaganda poster used during World War II to cast the entire Japanese people in a bad light. Almost always during wartime, governments create prejudicial messages to instill fear of the enemy and create support for the war effort.

seventy-five white men gathered to lynch the Stephensons. But blacks, many of them just returned from war, armed themselves and made it clear they were ready to die before allowing a lynching. They shouted out, "We fought for freedom overseas and we'll fight for it here!"

As the police and a white mob came running toward the blacks, they were met with gunfire. Early the next day, 500 National Guardsmen and 100 state troopers raided the black neighborhood. They smashed down doors, broke windows, chopped up furniture, and tore out rugs, claiming they were looking for concealed weapons.

There were many arrests of blacks—not whites—and two trials, with the NAACP's lawyers defending the accused. In the end, juries acquitted all but one of the twenty-five blacks charged with riot and attempted murder.

What happened in Tennessee in February 1946 showed how determined black veterans were to demand respect from whites. To NAACP leaders, it was a sign that a civil rights movement was emerging.

And the NAACP was ready for it. It had a group of lawyers who had been highly trained at Howard University's law school. Led by Charles Houston and Thurgood Marshall, they would attack the legal foundations that supported the structure of racial injustice in America. Their goal was the integration of African Americans into

Thurgood Marshall, chief counsel of the NAACP, standing on the steps of the Supreme Court, where he won several crucial cases in the drive for desegregation. Later he was appointed U.S. Solicitor General and Associate Justice of the U.S. Supreme Court.

the American mainstream. And they meant to use the courts, the press, and the ballot to that end.

What helped the civil rights movement was the rising tide of nonwhite peoples of the world. After World War II, they began to get together to demand that the Western world end the old white-dominated colonial order. By now the World War II alliance of the United States with Russia had ended. A Cold War had begun. When the United States pronounced itself "the leader of the free world," it was taunted by government leaders of the underdeveloped nations. What kind of free world leader is it, they asked, that treats its own black community as second-class citizens? That challenge from abroad

strengthened the position of American blacks as they bar-
gained for their rights. They were saying to the government, prove that America is not "unfree."

Soon there were signs of a gathering momentum
toward the protection of civil rights. In 1948, under pressure, President Harry Truman issued an executive order
ending segregation in the armed forces. It was the first
fruit of a presidential Commission on Civil Rights that
Truman had set up to study the problem and propose
measures for its solution. Its report called for "the elimi-
nation of segregation from American life."

In the 1948 election, the issue had become big
enough to split the Democratic Party. Henry Wallace, Vice
President under FDR, led a new Progressive Party calling
for full civil rights, while Strom Thurmond led the right
wing of the Democrats in a campaign for preservation of
the old Jim Crow style of living. Truman, picking up some
of Wallace's proposals, won.

Among the states, New York took the lead in protecting civil rights. In 1945 it passed America's first fair
employment practices law, with enforcement provisions.
Dozens of states eventually followed. And one, Connecti-
cut, became the first state to ban Jim Crow in housing.

But even as progress was being made, opposition,
both silent and violent, continued. Harry T. Moore and his
wife, NAACP leaders of a register-to-vote drive in

Florida, were killed in 1951 when their home was bombed.

Southern whites in those days liked to say that they lived in a good town, a "peaceful" town. Peaceful because no black had yet challenged the system of segregation and discrimination. But peace—never universal, always only on the surface—would be broken again and again as the 1950s opened.

Step by step, from the 1930s into the 1950s, the NAACP carried the fight for the franchise and for equal educational opportunities through the courts. (See pages 78–79 for a selected list of rulings.) Finally, on May 17, 1954, in a sweeping decision, the U.S. Supreme Court said that persons "required on the basis of race to attend separate schools were deprived of the equal protection of the law guaranteed by the Fourteenth Amendment."

The court had unanimously supported the parents of

Linda Brown of Topeka, Kansas. They wanted their daughter to be able to attend a white school four blocks from their home rather than having to go twenty-one blocks to

Nine-year-old Linda Brown in front of all-black Monroe Elementary School in Topeka, Kansas. She was the subject of the Supreme Court case that ended legal school segregation.

the black school to which she had been assigned. The court noted that the "separate but equal" doctrine had no place in public education because "separate educational facilities are inherently unequal." Playgrounds and bathrooms and textbooks in black schools were more decrepit and underfinanced than in white schools. Segregation in education, the justices believed, could only reinforce the feeling of inferiority already existing among blacks and could have permanent negative effects on the minds of black children.

Of course the Fourteenth Amendment, added to the Constitution in 1868, had declared all citizens were due the "equal protection of the laws." But it was dead almost from the day it was born; its true meaning had been ignored by the Supreme Court and never enforced by presidents.

It can't be said that the justices had suddenly seen the light or had a moral vision. No, they were responding to new pressures, to a changing world, to courageous black people fighting for equality and ready to risk their lives by carrying the issue into the courts. The people in local chapters of the NAACP were the flag-bearers, leading the way to justice for all.

There was jubilation at first. Millions of blacks rejoiced that at last—over ninety years after emancipation—basic civil rights for all were recognized. But resistance to the Court's ruling was voiced at once in the Deep South. A few months after the 1954 decision, a White Citizens Council composed of "more respectable" people than the Ku Klux Klan sprang up in Mississippi and spread rapidly. The leaders claimed they would use only legal means to fight the Court decision, but their methods went far beyond. Open and overt terror, brutal threats, economic reprisals against the few whites who supported desegregation—all were employed. Their tools were boycotts, job dismissals, denial of credit, and

Part of a crowd of 5,000 screaming mothers and children who have gathered before the New Orleans school board on November 16, 1960, to protest the desegregation of two schools. The meeting was organized by the White Citizens Council.

mortgage foreclosures. They also distributed leaflets and pamphlets to counter the civil rights movement.

In 1955, the Court, under intense pressure from Southerners, ordered all schools to proceed with desegregation "with all deliberate speed." It meant local schools could work out their own desegregation plans to suit their own notions of how and when to desegregate.

The next year a hundred Southern congressmen openly urged defiance of the law with a "Southern Manifesto." It denounced the *Brown* decision and called for

In Montgomery, Alabama, teenagers wave signs and Confederate flags as they demonstrate in 1963 against the desegregation of the public schools.

using every lawful means to reverse it. The effect was to slow down the already creeping pace of desegregation.

The pace of school desegregation was agonizingly slow. Ten years after the Court's decision, only 9.2 percent of the black students in the Southern and border states were attending desegregated classes. Not until the 1980s, pressed hard by the courts, black citizens, and world opinion, did the South dismantle its dual public school systems. But many whites then sent their children to private segregated schools to avoid the law. And in the North, as time passed, more segregation developed in the schools than in the once solidly segregated South. The old pattern of Jim Crow housing and school districts designed to keep blacks separate from whites managed

An angry white mother removes her child from Graymont School in Birmingham, Alabama, the day it is desegregated in 1963.

to create all-black ghetto schools in many big cities.

What would the federal government do to enforce the Court's ruling? President Dwight Eisenhower, who regretted he had appointed Chief Justice Earl Warren to the Court, said not a word in its support. The big test came in September 1957 when Governor Orval Faubus of Arkansas interfered with a court order directing Central High School in Little Rock to admit qualified black students.

THE LEGAL STRUGGLE

Some think that the civil rights movement started with the Supreme Court decision of 1954 in *Brown* v. *Board of Education of Topeka*. But as this book tries to show, its roots go much farther back. The modern legal struggle for civil rights, up to *Brown,* can be traced in this calendar of Supreme Court decisions:

1917. Residential segregation is declared unconstitutional in cities.

1936. The University of Maryland is ordered to admit a black applicant, Donald G. Murray, to its law school.

1938. Kentucky is ordered not to exclude people from jury lists solely because of their race or color.

1938. The University of Missouri is ordered to admit a black college student, Lloyd Gaines, to its law school.

1940. Forced confessions are outlawed.

1944. White primaries (which stipulated that only whites could vote in the primary nominating contests) are declared unconstitutional.

1946. Segregated seating is banned on buses in interstate travel.

1947. Any practice of excluding citizens on the basis of race from jury duty results in unconstitutional indictments and verdicts.

1948. Restrictive covenants (clauses in deeds of houses prohibiting their sale to people stereotyped as undesirable, such as blacks, Jews, or other ethnic and racial minorities) are declared unconstitutional.

1949. Confessions are invalid if coerced and the state has intentionally kept blacks off the jury.

1950. An all-white school is compelled to admit a black student despite the "separate but equal" law.

1953. Any "respectable, well-behaved person" has a right to be served in any public place in Washington, D.C.

CHAPTER 9

Central High in Little Rock

WHEN CENTRAL HIGH SCHOOL OPENED on September 4, 1957, 250 armed National Guardsmen surrounded the building. Why? To ensure that the nine black boys and girls scheduled to enter the school would be safe?

No. Arkansas Governor Orval Faubus had announced on TV that he was sending the National Guard to keep *out* the black students. If any attempt at integrating the school was made, he warned, "blood will run in the streets."

Early that morning, eight of the students had met at the home of Daisy Bates, editor and head of the state NAACP, so they could ride to school together in her car. But the ninth, Elizabeth Eckford, arrived alone at Central High, to

Elizabeth Eckford braves a white mob as she enters Central High in Little Rock, Arkansas, when the desegregated school opens for the year in 1957.

find a white mob screaming at her and shouting, "Lynch her!"

A white woman stepped in and led Elizabeth away. When the eight other students neared the school, they turned back at the sight of the mob.

This opposition had been unexpected. Little Rock was considered a moderate Southern city, outside the Deep South. It had also proposed a desegregation plan approved by the federal courts. But on the day before the school session was to start, the governor decided to oppose desegregation. His TV address and the hysteria whipped up by white racists led to mob action against anyone who appeared to be sympathetic to the teenage students. Reporters were kicked and beaten while police stood by. The Bates home was bombed and sprayed with bullets at night, its windows were smashed, and crosses were burned on the lawn.

This was the first time a Southern governor had used state troops to defy the *Brown* decision. Although a

White students block the door to Little Rock's high school as African American students try to enter on the day a federal judge's desegregation order takes effect.

federal judge in Arkansas ruled that the school integration plan should proceed, Governor Faubus again sent the National Guard to block the black students from entering Central. Realizing this was now a political issue, the NAACP called on President Eisenhower to federalize the National Guard and take command away from Faubus.

Eisenhower, however, was reluctant to take action. Days passed with Faubus urging the president to defy the Court. Eisenhower did nothing. Finally, Faubus obeyed another court order not to use the troops to keep out the black students. On September 23 the nine were rushed into Central under police guard. But an angry white mob of over a thousand rioted outside, attacking reporters and black passersby. The police chief could not control the situation and ordered the black students to be packed in cars and secretly driven away.

Mobs near the school kept beating up any black they could lay their hands on. The city's mayor telegrammed the president to say that Faubus was behind the mob violence and had helped organize it. As the situation grew more violent, the mayor again wired the president, begging for federal troops to take control "in the interest of humanity, law and order, and democracy worldwide. . . ." This time the president acted. He ordered the 101st Airborne Division from Fort Campbell in Kentucky to go to Little Rock. A thousand paratroopers arrived to assure the safety of the black students. They circled the school and escorted the black children in the hallways. The president also placed 10,000 members of the Arkansas National Guard on special federal service.

Only when President Eisenhower ordered federal troops to protect black students seeking to enter Little Rock's Central High did they succeed in taking their seats in class.

After two months, the paratroopers and most of the Guardsmen were removed. A small number remained on federal duty until the school year ended, with Central graduating its first black student, Ernest Green. But upon request of the Little Rock school board, a federal judge ordered that school integration be delayed for two years, because of threats of more violence. That ruling in time was overturned by the Supreme Court. The public schools were not reopened until the fall of 1959. Racists would keep violence and disorder alive in Little Rock for years. By 1962 all the formerly all-white high schools in the city were desegregated.

Progress in gaining civil rights continued. By the early 1980s Little Rock had an African American mayor and city manager. The director of human resources for the city was black. Five blacks sat in the state legislature. And 53 percent of Central High's students were black.

Southeast of Little Rock, in Montgomery, Alabama, another form of struggle for civil rights—mass nonviolent action—had begun and was already creating headlines around the world.

ERNEST GREEN'S DIPLOMA

Sixteen-year-old Ernest Green was the first black to graduate from Central High in Little Rock. It was June 1958. To be that "first" took extraordinary guts for the young African American, for there were so many "first things" blacks had yet to be permitted to do in their own country. Langston Hughes, the poet of his people, wrote a tribute to Green in a column for the *Chicago Defender.* In it he said:

Ernest Green on graduation day.

In some parts of our country just average day-to-day living needs from Negroes more courage and determination than it does from whites. When something a little out of the ordinary is done, it may call for heroics.

Teenager Ernest Green took his life in his hands to get that diploma. He walked through mobs, endured spit and curses, braved brickbats, and passed lines of soldiers with unsure bayonets to get that diploma.

In the classroom he suffered whispered threats from unfriendly students, and in the halls intentional pushing and ugly jeering, but he got his diploma. To graduate was his determination. He did—and so became THE MAN OF THE YEAR for 1958.

And in that diploma are the hopes and dreams of millions of Negroes long dead who never got an education. The dim wonder of "book learning" in the minds of countless slaves who dared not touch a book for fear of flogging lies in that diploma.

The blood of young black men and women beaten by overseers until their backs were raw for daring to study in secret is soaked into the paper of that diploma. The tears of slave mothers who desperately wanted their children to learn moisten all the letters on Ernest Green's diploma.

His diploma is no ordinary diploma. No! It is the diploma of all the people who remember grandfathers and grandmothers who did not know how to read and write because they never had a chance to learn, for whom the barriers to learning were too high, or the terrors in the way too great.

Out of so many years of struggle, this sixteen-year-old graduate becomes 1958's MAN OF THE YEAR.

CHAPTER 10

Bus Boycott in Montgomery

THE TIME IS THURSDAY, DECEMBER 1, 1955—two years before the events at Little Rock.

That evening, Rosa Parks, an African American seamstress, coming home from work at a downtown department store, boards a bus for home. She pays her fare, sees a vacant seat in the middle of the bus, and takes it. At the next stop, some whites get on and fill up the "white" seats in the front. One of the whites is left standing. The driver looks back and orders Mrs. Parks to stand up and move to the Jim Crow section of the bus in the rear so the man can sit. She does not move.

"Are you going to stand up?" the driver asks. "No," she says. "Well," he says, "I'm going to have you arrested." "You do that," she says. The driver gets out of the bus and waits for police to show up.

"As I sat there," Parks recalled, "I tried not to think about what might happen. I knew that anything was possible. I could be manhandled or beaten. I could be arrested. People have asked me if it occurred to me that I might be the test case the NAACP had been looking for. I did not think about that at all. In fact, if I let myself think too deeply about what might happen to me, I might have gotten off the bus. But I chose to remain."

Eventually, two policemen came. They got on the bus, and one of them asked her why she didn't stand up. She asked him, "Why do you all push us around?" He said to her, "I don't know, but the law is the law and you're under arrest."

Rosa Parks has been incorrectly described as an old woman who was too tired to move. She was forty-two at the time, college-educated, a committed activist, and secretary of the local NAACP. A dozen years earlier, in 1943, the very same bus driver had ordered her to move to the back and, when she refused, had forced her off the bus. (The drivers carried guns and had police power to enforce regulations.)

Now, in 1955, Parks was ready to carry the protest against Jim Crow to the end. "It was a matter of dignity," she said. "I could not have faced myself and my people if

Mrs. Rosa Parks being fingerprinted by a deputy sheriff in Montgomery, Alabama, where she was arrested for refusing to give up her bus seat to a white passenger.

I had moved." She called E. D. Nixon for help. He was a leader of the Brotherhood of Sleeping Car Porters and of the state NAACP as well. He bailed her out. The next morning, he phoned Ralph Abernathy, pastor of the First Baptist Church of Montgomery, and suggested a one-day boycott of city buses.

No Jim Crow law in Montgomery angered blacks more than bus segregation. They made up about two-thirds of the city's bus riders. They were forced to put up with humiliating rules, such as that they board the bus in the back, sit in the back of the bus, and give up their seats to any whites who were standing. A boycott—refusal to do business with the bus company—would reduce its profit and make it think twice about Jim Crow rules.

Abernathy agreed to Nixon's proposal. The Rev. Martin Luther King, Jr., pastor of the Dexter Avenue Baptist Church, made his church basement available for a meeting that evening to discuss the proposal.

King, twenty-six years old, was the newest minister in Montgomery. He had recently completed his doctoral studies at Boston University, and this church was his first pastoral assignment.

About forty black community leaders came to the meeting and endorsed a one-day boycott for the following Monday. Black taxi companies agreed to help by carrying the boycotters for ten cents, the usual bus fare. Blacks passed out leaflets about the boycott and the conservative local paper helped promote it inadvertently by printing the leaflet on the front page. On Sunday morning, every black pulpit sounded the call for the boycott. When King drove around town Monday morning in the early rush hours, he saw only eight blacks riding the buses. The boycott was a success! "A miracle had taken place," King said. "The once dormant and quiescent Negro community was now fully awake."

In police court that morning, Mrs. Parks was found

guilty of disobeying the city segregation ordinance and fined $10. She appealed the case, which made it a test of the validity of the segregation law itself. In the afternoon, several black leaders met to plan for the mass meeting scheduled for that evening. They formed the Montgomery Improvement Association (MIA) and elected King its president.

The group proposed, and the mass meeting would approve, continuing the boycott. The goal was modest—not complete integration, but only a more flexible color line. People would be seated on a first-come, first-served basis, with blacks filling seats from the rear forward and whites filling seats from the front back. And black bus drivers would be employed on predominantly black routes.

That night the meeting was packed, with the audience standing to sing "Onward, Christian Soldiers." Then King rose to speak, with TV cameras shooting from all sides. He spoke without manuscript or notes:

You know, my friends, there comes a time when people get tired of being trampled over by the iron feet of oppression. There comes a time, my friends, when people get tired of being plunged across the abyss of humiliation, where they experience the bleakness of nagging despair. There comes a time when people get

*tired of being pushed out of the glittering sunlight of
life's July, and left standing amid the piercing chill of an
alpine November.*

*And we are not wrong. We are not wrong in what
we are doing. If we are wrong, the Supreme Court of this
nation is wrong. If we are wrong, the Constitution of the
United States is wrong. If we are wrong, God Almighty is
wrong. If we are wrong, Jesus of Nazareth was merely a
utopian dreamer that never came down to earth. And we
are determined here in Montgomery to work and fight
until justice runs down like water and righteousness like
a mighty stream.*

*I want to say that in all our actions we must stick
together. Unity is the great need of the hour, and if we
are united we can get many of the things that we not
only desire but which we justly deserve. And don't let
anybody frighten you. We are not afraid of what we are
doing, because we are doing it within the law. There is
never a time in our American democracy that we must
ever think we're wrong when we protest. We reserve that
right. . . .*

When King finished, the people rose to their feet
and applauded. Nothing he had ever said before had
evoked so emotional a response. He realized for the first
time what older preachers meant when they said, "Open

your mouth and God will speak for you." As they voted to continue the boycott, cheers rang out from both inside and outside the church, where the overflow crowd was standing.

The problem of transport in the early days of the boycott was difficult. The city ruled that by law black cab drivers too had to charge the minimum fare of forty-five cents. That ended the cheap taxi service. But volunteers responded at once to an appeal for car-pooling. Hundreds offered their cars for use, mornings and evenings or all day. White housewives, no matter how committed to segregation, unexpectedly decided they would not do without their maids. Many of them drove to pick them up and take them home.

At first it was the Sermon on the Mount, Christian love, that guided the protest movement. But only a week into the boycott, a white woman who supported it wrote a letter to the newspaper comparing the bus protest with the Gandhian movement in India. And people who had never heard of Gandhi before began to see nonviolent resistance as a powerful weapon in the struggle for freedom. Though some of the blacks disagreed with it, the vast majority were willing to try the experiment.

To Martin Luther King, however, it was not just a convenient strategy for the moment but "a way of life that men live by because of the sheer morality of its claim." He had studied the concept at Crozer Seminary while reading of Gandhi's nonviolent opposition to British colonial rule in the 1940s.

Both city and bus officials expected the boycott to fizzle out in a short while. But it went on day after day, week after week. The bus company and the city could not help but feel the effect of 42,000 people refusing to ride city buses. Finally, they decided to negotiate. The first attempts got nowhere. Then some whites tried to sow dissension among the blacks, to conquer by dividing. That failed too. The city fathers, some of them publicly joining the White Citizens Council, tried a get-tough policy. They had blacks arrested for minor imaginary traffic violations. King too was arrested on a false speeding charge and jailed. As word of his arrest spread, a large crowd gathered outside, and the jailer, panicking, let King go.

Threatening letters flooded King's mailbox. He began to fear violence, assassination. One night, when he was not at home, a bomb exploded on his porch. Luckily, his wife and little daughter were not injured. When they heard the news, hundreds of angry blacks rushed to King's home. Many came with sticks, rocks, bottles, knives, guns. King feared nonviolent resistance was on the verge of ending. He spoke to the crowd, assured them his family was unharmed, and urged them not to panic or pick up weapons. "He who lives by the sword will perish by the

The Rev. Martin Luther King, Jr., is manhandled by Montgomery police as they book him on charges of "loitering."

sword," he reminded them. "We cannot solve the problem through retaliatory violence. We must love our white brothers no matter what they do to us. We must meet hate with love. What we are doing is just, and God is with us." No matter what happened to him, he said, "this movement will not stop."

The boycott went on. The company was forced to raise fares and cut schedules to reduce its losses. Downtown stores were losing business because fewer blacks were coming in to shop.

The bus company decided it would grant the MIA's

demands if the city would repeal the bus segregation ordinance. An influential group of businessmen tried to get the city to agree. But the mayor (a member of the White Citizens Council) said he didn't care if blacks never rode the buses again.

Two nights after King's home was bombed, a stick of dynamite exploded on E. D. Nixon's lawn. A third bombing occurred at the home of a white pastor who was secretary of the MIA. But the violence did not halt the movement or provoke violence in response. It only further solidified the cause and brought sympathy for it from people of goodwill around the world.

Meanwhile, the NAACP's lawyers challenged bus segregation in the courts. In June 1956 a federal district court called bus segregation within a state unconstitutional. The city of Montgomery appealed. But the U.S. Supreme Court unanimously upheld the lower court's decision on November 13, 1956. And five weeks later, the ruling took effect. The mayor said he would obey the desegregation law, and the company instructed its drivers to be courteous.

It was fifty-five weeks after Rosa Parks's arrest. King became the first passenger to ride an integrated city bus in Montgomery, Alabama. Soon after, early in 1957, in the wake of the successful bus boycott, King and other activist ministers founded the Southern Christian

Leadership Conference (SCLC). King was chosen president. It became the leader in organizing nonviolent demonstrations for civil rights all over the South.

WHY DIRECT ACTION?

As the movement's tactics developed, some people were at first confused about the principle of nonviolence. They didn't see that the word "resistance" was coupled with it and that "direct action" was a form of resistance. Martin Luther King spoke to the puzzled ones in this passage from his "Letter from Birmingham Jail":

You may well ask: "Why direct action? Why sit-ins, marches, and so forth? Isn't negotiation a better path?" You are quite right in calling for negotiation. Indeed, this is the very purpose of direct action. Nonviolent direct action seeks to create such a crisis and foster such a tension that a community which has constantly refused to negotiate is forced to confront the issue. It seeks to dramatize the issue so that it can no longer be ignored. My citing the creation of tension as part of the work of the nonviolent resister may sound rather shocking. But I must confess that I am not afraid of the word "tension." I have earnestly opposed violent tension, but there is a type of constructive, nonviolent tension which is necessary for growth. Just as Socrates felt that it was necessary to create a tension in the mind so that individuals could rise from the bondage of myths and half-truths to the unfettered realm of creative analysis and objective appraisal, so must we see the need for nonviolent gadflies to create the kind of tension in society that will help men rise from the dark depths of prejudice and racism to the majestic heights of understanding and brotherhood. . . .

Students from St. Augustine College in Raleigh, North Carolina, refused service at a lunch counter for whites only, study while conducting their sit-in protest.

CHAPTER 11

Sit-ins and Freedom Rides

WHAT HAPPENED IN MONTGOMERY marked a new beginning in the struggle that had been going on since the first slave ships reached the shores of America. The nation's claim to be democratic, to assure all its citizens of the right to life, liberty, and the pursuit of happiness, had met the first mass challenge to live up to that vision.

Out of the bus boycott came something new—nonviolent resistance—that people of any color, creed, or class would find enormously helpful in bringing about social change. It was a way to serve moral ends with moral means.

As for African Americans themselves, in Montgomery, they showed the world they could organize brilliantly and work courageously and collectively to reach their goals. The old passivity was gone. An exuberant new sense of dignity and destiny replaced it.

Remember those four teenage students who in February 1960 sat in at the Woolworth's lunch counter in Greensboro, North Carolina? The news from Greensboro hit home for that whole generation of black students. The pictures on television of the Greensboro sit-in galvanized many of them into action. Robert Moses and Julian Bond, soon to be youth leaders of the movement, said that what they saw on the TV screen changed their lives. Liberal white students too joined with blacks to work for social change.

In the first two weeks after Greensboro, there were sit-ins against segregation laws in fifteen other Southern cities. By April, it was seventy-eight cities, and by the year's end, 70,000 people had taken part in demonstrations. And 3,600 of them had gone to jail for their beliefs. Like the black people of Montgomery, they too had risen up.

Old feelings and customs were disrupted by these sudden sit-ins for the right to buy a hot dog or a hamburger at the same lunch counter with whites. Dime stores and department stores, train and bus terminals felt the effects of student sit-ins. Soon they spread to become read-ins in public libraries, wade-ins in municipal

Young African American demonstrators, arrested in 1962 for parading without a permit, kneel in prayer on a sidewalk in Albany, Georgia.

swimming pools, kneel-ins at churches, and stand-ins at movie theaters that barred blacks.

Always peaceful? No. In Jacksonville, Florida, reported the *New York Times*, "Whites armed with ax handles, baseball bats, and other weapons set upon black youth. Intermittent rioting followed. Other riots have taken place in Portsmouth, Virginia, and Chattanooga, Tennessee. There have been mass arrests in many Southern cities."

Most sit-in leaders followed the pattern of nonviolent action developed by Dr. King. The objective, he said, "was not to coerce but to correct; not to break wills or bodies, but to move hearts."

It was teenagers who led the way. At that time, the great majority of black students were the first in their families to go to college, North or South. In their class-rooms, in their dorms, the focus of talk was on the gross contradiction between what America proclaimed it stood for and what it actually practiced. Anyone with a smidgen of knowledge about American history might well wonder, How come anyone had to sit in at a "whites-only" lunch

Although the Fifteenth Amendment, adopted in 1870, guaranteed African Ameri-cans the right to vote, it was totally ignored in the South after Reconstruction. Here black students demonstrate in 1963 in front of a casket containing a copy of the amendment.

counter and get arrested? Why should sit-ins be needed to end Jim Crow in public places throughout the South? Didn't the Thirteenth Amendment end not only slavery but all the stigmas of slavery? Surely, the Fourteenth Amendment meant what it said: that "the citizens of the United States shall be entitled to all privileges and immunities of citizens in the several States."

Well, time to stop wondering and act. The newfound confidence of the student activists led to the formation of an organization called the Student Nonviolent Coordinating Committee (SNCC). These young people were often the spearhead of the civil rights movement in the Deep South. They worked together with others—the NAACP, CORE, and SCLC—while retaining their independence.

Three civil rights leaders join in a demonstration in Canton, Mississippi, in 1966. From left: Martin Luther King, Jr., Floyd McKissick of CORE, and Stokely Carmichael of SNCC.

The civil rights movement, by now so deep and so broad, influenced the 1960 presidential contest between John F. Kennedy and Richard M. Nixon. Neither candidate could ignore the civil rights issue. Kennedy won by the narrowest of margins, helped by the large black vote he got. But as president, he did not at first push for any major civil rights measures. Later, however, under increasing pressure from the movement, he would support the struggle for federal civil rights laws.

There was support from the Supreme Court too. In 1961 Thurgood Marshall filed an NAACP brief arguing that the Fourteenth Amendment gave the students the right to be served in a public restaurant. The Court agreed. The sit-ins had succeeded.

But there were still other barriers to be broken down. Many years before, in 1946, the Supreme Court had declared that segregation was unconstitutional on interstate transport. And in December 1960 it had ruled that segregation in station rooms, waiting rooms, and lunchrooms was illegal too. But would that decision be enforced? CORE decided to test the new ruling with a "Freedom Ride."

On May 4, 1961, thirteen people—seven young blacks and six older whites—left Washington aboard two buses, headed for New Orleans. As their buses rolled south through Virginia and North Carolina, the Freedom

Freedom Riders conduct a sit-in in 1961 at a waiting room reserved for white customers at the bus terminal in Montgomery, Alabama.

Riders, black and white, integrated waiting rooms and lunch counters successfully and usually without incident. In South Carolina, however, two of the Riders were beaten by a white mob, and the next day two others were arrested at a lunchroom in that state. A mob tried, but failed, to storm the jail holding them, and at dawn the next day the men were quietly released.

On May 14 a mob armed with chains, sticks, and iron rods met one of the buses as it pulled into the station at Anniston, Alabama. The mob attacked the bus, smashed its windows, slashed the front tires. Several hours later, the mob intercepted the Freedom Riders again, several miles out of town, and someone threw an incendiary bomb into the bus. The bus burst into flames, but the passengers were able to get out and were treated for smoke inhalation at a nearby hospital.

When this bus carrying black and white Freedom Riders in 1961 reached Anniston, Alabama, a white mob set the bus afire, slashed its tires, and attacked the passengers.

When the second group of Freedom Riders pulled into Anniston on the other bus, again a mob awaited them. They beat two of the men so badly that one suffered a stroke, which paralyzed him. When the bus reached Birmingham, again a mob attacked, with one rider so injured he required fifty-three stitches in his face and head.

Both groups of Freedom Riders wanted to go on, but frightened bus drivers refused to drive them out of Birmingham.

Six days later, another group, mostly SNCC members, continued the Freedom Ride from Birmingham. But only after federal authorities assured the bus company of protection. The new Riders were arrested and jailed in Mississippi for trying to integrate bus stations. That only made more people volunteer to be Freedom Riders. By summer's end, hundreds from all over the country had joined on Freedom Rides. In Jackson, Mississippi, 328 of them were arrested and jailed.

Violence against them was unrestrained. Often, it seemed to have the approval of National Guard units and local police. FBI agents stood by, took notes, did nothing. Federal marshals sent by Washington to protect the civil rights of Freedom Riders were threatened with arrest by Alabama's governor, John Patterson. "We do not recognize the federal marshals as law enforcement officers in this matter," he said. Next door in Mississippi, Governor

Two Freedom Riders—John Lewis (left) and James Zwerg—were brutally beaten by whites when they rode a Greyhound bus into Montgomery, Alabama, in 1961. (Lewis was later elected a U.S. Congressman from Georgia.)

Ross Barnett declared, "Integration will ruin civilization." At Jackson, officers with police dogs arrested Freedom Riders as soon as they stepped off buses. They sentenced twenty-seven of them to sixty days in the notorious Parchman prison farm, designed for hardened criminals.

The media—newspapers, magazines, television— had sent reporters and photographers to cover the rapidly growing mass protests in the South. What the nation saw in the press and on television shocked great numbers of people in the North. It took that impact on public opinion to get the federal government to do at least a little something. In November 1961 the Interstate Commerce Commission issued regulations that posters must be put up in all interstate terminals establishing the right of travel without segregation.

The Freedom Riders had made a difference. A number of bus and railroad stations in the South integrated their facilities. Many WHITE and COLORED signs were taken down and seats anywhere in a public bus made open to all. Still, compliance was not universal. Two years later, in Winona, Mississippi, blacks who used the white waiting room were arrested and savagely beaten.

The Freedom Rides and sit-ins had a double effect on the movement and its opposition. Civil rights had now drawn the support of many whites, including ministers and rabbis. On the other hand, Southern politicians learned they could gain advantage by campaigning against the civil rights movement.

When the Supreme Court ordered the desegregation of Alabama schools in 1963, the Ku Klux Klan and the White Citizens Councils went into the streets in protest.

Many in the Kennedy Administration, while probably in favor of desegregation, feared alienating Southerners in the Congress. Yet they knew how badly they needed black votes if Kennedy was to win reelection in 1964.

For President Kennedy, civil rights was a minefield. He was trying to balance appeals to white Southerners and to blacks. The white South was his party's traditional base. If he made a strong commitment to civil rights, he might permanently lose the white South.

Not that Kennedy didn't think racism was wrong. But he felt no moral passion about it. From his election on, he tried to keep a low profile on civil rights. The sit-ins and Freedom Rides that uncovered the brutality of Southern racism forced him to do something. No, he did not broadcast to the nation a powerful denunciation of the evils of segregation. Instead, he maneuvered behind the scenes to avoid more civil rights confrontations.

It was now that the movement decided on a massive campaign to register black voters in the Deep South. The Kennedy Administration quietly approved of the plan and suggested that liberal foundations might help finance such an effort.

GO SLOW? WAIT?

Even white clergymen sympathetic to the movement were upset by the furious pressure of the black community to end segregation and injustice *now*. So many marches, sit-ins, Freedom Rides, demonstrations! Go slow, some said, wait. Give the authorities time to change things. Wait? said Martin Luther King. How long?

We have waited for more than 340 years for our constitutional and God-given rights. The nations of Asia and Africa are moving with jetlike speed toward gaining political independence, but we still creep at horse-and-buggy pace toward gaining a cup of coffee at a

Dorothy Bell, 19, a college student in Birmingham, Alabama, waits at a downtown lunch counter for service that would never come. In 1963 she and twenty others were arrested for their sit-ins.

lunch counter. Perhaps it is easy for those who have never felt the stinging darts of segregation to say, "Wait." But when you have seen vicious mobs lynch your mothers and fathers at will and drown your sisters and brothers at whim; when you have seen hate-filled policemen curse, kick, and even kill your black brothers and sisters; when you see the vast majority of your twenty million Negro brothers smothering in an airtight cage of poverty in the midst of an affluent society; when you suddenly find your tongue twisted and your speech stammering as you seek to explain to your six-year-old daughter why she can't go to the public amusement park that has just been advertised on television, and see tears welling up in her eyes when she is told that Funtown is closed to colored children, and see ominous clouds of inferiority beginning to form in her little mental sky, and see her beginning to distort her personality by developing an unconscious bitterness toward white people; when you have to concoct an answer for a five-year-old son who is asking: "Daddy, why do white people treat colored people so mean?"; when you take a cross-country drive and find it necessary to sleep night after night in the uncomfortable corners of your automobile because no motel will accept you; when you are humiliated day in and day out by nagging signs reading "white" and "colored"; when your first name becomes "nigger," your middle name becomes "boy" (however old you are), and your last name becomes "John," and your wife and mother are never given the respected title "Mrs."; when you are harried by day and haunted by night by the fact that you are a Negro, living constantly at tiptoe stance, never quite knowing what to expect next, and are plagued with inner fears and outer resentments; when you are forever fighting a degenerating sense of "nobodiness"—then you will understand why we find it difficult to wait. There comes a time when the cup of endurance runs over, and men are no longer willing to be plunged into the abyss of despair. I hope, sirs, you can understand our legitimate and unavoidable impatience.

CHAPTER 12

I Ain't Scared of Your Jail!

A WAVE OF VOTER REGISTRATION DRIVES swept across the South. Why had it been so difficult for blacks to register and vote? Take Selma, Alabama. At that time, out of 15,000 blacks of voting age in the town and the surrounding Dallas County, only a few hundred were registered. The most basic barrier to the ballot box was fear, fear produced by 350 years of slavery and segregation. Fear of the gun and the club in the hands of Gestapo-like police and sheriffs. Yet the right to vote was vital to a people hungry for a voice in their destiny.

In thousands of communities, local and county government was controlled by segregationist officials who put up every possible roadblock to the ballot box. A literacy test designed to be very difficult was one of the main tools used.

Sometimes educated blacks were told that they had failed the test. Then when they asked "How come? In what way have we made mistakes?" the answer was "We can't tell you; the results are confidential." Another block was the deliberately slow pace of the registrar and the limited number of days and hours during which the office was open.

Led by Martin Luther King, Jr., African Americans in February 1965 line up in front of the county courthouse in Selma, Alabama, determined to register to vote.

It seemed little or nothing could be done about it while the machinery for enforcing this basic right of citizenship was in the control of state-appointed officials. They knew that only so long as they kept the blacks from voting could they continue to hold the reins of power. How to plug up the loopholes, expose the deceitful and irregular practice? It could only be done if the federal government were forced to take control from the states or to set up the machinery for the effective policing of registering and voting. There had been some legal reforms in 1957, 1960, and 1964, but it was only piecemeal and poorly enforced.

By now Martin Luther King had become a kind of roving leader. Local movements springing up all over the South would call him for help. They knew he could inspire their people to greater efforts. His presence guaranteed that the national media would cover their actions. Since Montgomery, he had developed connections with religious, educational, and labor groups that could mobilize "people of goodwill" to come help in the struggle.

The communities knew too that King himself would lead marches and go to jail. The staff of the SCLC, his organization, could offer experienced help to those new to the movement. So in the small town of Albany, Georgia, where 22,000 blacks lived, when SNCC workers and the local NAACP launched a movement not only for voter registration but to challenge the whole system of segregation, they asked King to come help.

On December 16, 1961, more than 700 people demonstrating for voting rights, led by King, were arrested in Albany. Protest continued, with people coming out of mass meetings in the churches singing "We Shall Overcome," "Ain't Gonna Let Nobody Turn Me 'Round," and "This Little Light of Mine." They went into jail, singing and praying. The police threatened them: "Cut out that singing and praying!" But they kept on and on and on. Out of Albany's jails came the dynamic SNCC Freedom Singers, whose music rang out across the nation and over the world . . . "Woke up this morning with my mind stayed on Freedom. . . ." The mass demonstrations continued. Two more times King was arrested, freed soon on bail or with suspended sentence. When it became plain that the civil rights movement would no longer accept the denial of so basic a right, the registration drives, like the sit-ins and Freedom Rides, were often met with violent resistance. Howard Zinn, a history professor at Spelman College, Atlanta, was sent to Albany to report on what was happening there:

I found that blacks were doing no more than exercising their constitutional rights—marching, assembling, and speaking. Yet they were jailed and beaten—a pregnant

black woman was kicked and lost her baby, a white civil
rights worker had his jaw broken, a black lawyer was
clubbed bloody by the local sheriff—and the U.S.
government did nothing to interfere.

I knew what the Constitution said, and that was
enough to make me sure President Kennedy and his
brother, Attorney General Robert Kennedy, were not
abiding by their oaths of office. I looked up the statutes.

After dragging a young
black man from a seg-
regated lunch counter
in 1963 in Jackson,
Mississippi, where he
was waiting to be
served, a white man
has hurled him to the
ground and viciously
kicks him as a crowd
stands by, cheering on
the assault.

119

There was a law passed after the Civil War, now in the books as Title 18, Section 242 of the U.S. Code, which made it a crime for any official to willfully deprive any persons of their constitutional rights. That law was not being used to protect blacks in the South.

Activists faced not only physical hardship but punishment by other means. Many Southern teachers who took part in voter registration were fired by their school boards. Whole communities of black tenant farmers were evicted in rural Tennessee. In Bessemer, Alabama, a black union leader received six months on the chain gang for ordering a poster with the words VOTE TODAY FOR A BETTER TOMORROW.

During the voting drive in Georgia in 1962, eight black churches housing voter registration meetings were bombed or burned by terrorists. Still, in the face of such violent opposition, some progress was made. In 1962 the Supreme Court ordered reapportionment of a voting district so that blacks would have a fairer chance to gain representation in office. And black voters in Georgia elected an African American to the state senate. The first time in more than fifty years! That victory encouraged the campaigners to redouble their efforts everywhere in the South.

The people of Albany, black and white, and the movement itself were changed in profound ways. The blacks would never be shoved back to the time before 1961, nor would the whites ever see things in the same old way.

Where would the civil rights movement go from there? To Birmingham, Alabama—the most segregated city in America. Like Mississippi, it had a reputation—bloody, frightening—as a terrible place for black people. Some called the city "Bombingham" because whites had always been ready to destroy any black movement toward civil rights and freedom. What African American didn't know of someone who had been hounded out of town, beaten, or killed for resisting a system so much like the old system of racial separation in South Africa, called "apartheid"?

The Rev. Fred Shuttlesworth was one of those everybody in Birmingham knew about. They had never scared him out of town, although they had beaten him and almost killed him. So when Shuttlesworth asked King to come to Birmingham in the spring of 1963, he came.

Within a week after King led the first demonstrations for voting rights in the streets, he knew this would be the hardest time the movement had ever faced. Birmingham was "bigger and badder" than Albany or Montgomery. In the young blacks of the city, King recognized great forces of energy and a readiness to take on whatever white authority could do and to overcome it. Thousands of children and youth marched in the streets, against swinging clubs and snarling police dogs and jets of fire hoses that swept them off their feet and hurled them into the distance. For five days running, the TV scenes of police brutality reached around the world. This was the battleground of Eugene "Bull" Connor, the brutal racist who commanded the police.

Birmingham firemen turn their power hoses full force against civil rights demonstrators in July 1963. The Alabama city was a focal point of the desegregation movement.

On April 12, Good Friday, King was arrested for leading a march into the city. Over the Easter weekend, he wrote his great "Letter from Birmingham Jail." It was a passionate denunciation of those who asked black people to wait, to slow down, to take it easy for a while. And as passionate an argument for the morality of breaking unjust laws.

Martin Luther King, Jr., during the nine days he was confined in the Birmingham city jail.

As King was placed in solitary confinement, his wife called the White House, and President Kennedy himself phoned back to promise help. His brother, Attorney General Robert Kennedy, called Birmingham officials and King was released from jail. The Kennedy Administration, which had shelved civil rights legislation, now put a strong bill at the top of its congressional program. Birmingham committed Kennedy to doing what he could to meet the demands of the movement.

On May 2 a national audience watched on TV as

over a thousand black children, some only six years old, marched out of church to demonstrate on the street. They sang freedom songs, chanted freedom slogans, and kneeled on the pavement to pray as the police rounded them up and poured them into patrol wagons to be taken to jail. None cried, they only laughed and skipped and danced as the police collared them.

Putting children on the firing line? Was that right? King answered that by demonstrating the children gained "a sense of their own stake in freedom and justice." Here they were, showing the whole world their pride in their people and their readiness to shape their own future.

On May 3 another demonstration took place. "Bull" Connor's police charged into a park where the demonstrators gathered, swinging clubs against anyone in sight, demonstrators or onlookers. Again, attack dogs were loosed against fleeing boys and girls. Again, firemen with high-pressure hoses blasted blacks against buildings and swept children down slippery streets. The water pressure was powerful enough to rip the bark off trees, tear the clothes off people's backs, cut through their skin. At the close of these two days of demonstration, nearly 1,300 blacks were in jail.

On the morning of May 6, leaflets handed out near black schools urged all the students: "Fight for freedom first. Then go to school. Join the thousands in jail who are

As civil rights demonstrators in Birmingham flee the punishing force of firemen's hoses, a boy turns to confront his attackers.

making their witness for freedom. Come to the Sixteenth Street Baptist Church now . . . and we'll soon be freed. It's up to you to free our teachers, our parents, yourself, and our country."

The response of the kids was overwhelming. In some schools that day, attendance was 90 percent off. As the young demonstrators left the church, the police hustled them into the waiting patrol wagons. The charge was "parading without a permit." The students went, singing: "I ain't scared of your jail/'cause I want my freedom/want my freedom/want my freedom now." Hour after hour, waves of students offered themselves up for arrest. The courage of these boys and girls only enraged Connor the more. As TV cameras and photographers recorded it, police dogs, fire hoses, and clubs again savaged the children and the adults watching them.

On May 7 the movement mounted to its climax. Waves of black men and women were again ready to march against Connor's police, this time reinforced by hundreds of Governor George Wallace's state troopers. And now, on the edge of a tragic crisis, the Kennedy Administration intervened. It persuaded Birmingham's business leadership to reach a desegregation accord with King and Shuttlesworth just in time to prevent what could have been a massacre. Three days later, in front of the Gaston Motel, a jubilant King announced that the Birmingham power structure had accepted the movement's demands.

Black nonviolence had won concessions. But white violence did not give up. The Gaston Motel, where King was staying, was bombed by white extremists, and so was the home nearby of King's brother, the Rev. A. D. King. A dynamite blast killed four young black girls in a Baptist Sunday school. Police killed another child on the street, and white boys killed a black boy riding on his bicycle.

In the ten weeks after the demonstrations in Birmingham, there were over 750 demonstrations in seventy-five Southern cities, with some 3,000 people arrested. By the end of 1963, protests had taken place in 800 cities across the country.

This large crater in the basement of a Birmingham Baptist church was created on September 15, 1963, when a dynamite blast set off by white supremacists killed four black girls.

As more and more people, black and white, joined together that year in the struggle for civil rights, A. Philip Randolph proposed that all the forces on that front be united in one great dramatic action—a March on Washington. The movement had shown it could organize effectively in the communities. But it had never aimed for a national gathering of such giant proportions. The aim was to call upon Congress to pass the Kennedy civil rights bill and to highlight the economic discrimination blacks suffered as well.

At first, the Kennedy people wondered how wise it was. Would it only provoke Southern congressmen to intensify their opposition to the pending civil rights bill? But the powerful momentum of the protest movement that spring and summer made JFK realize it could not be stopped. So he would use it to muster still more support for his civil rights bill.

On August 28 more than 250,000 people, black and white, people of all faiths, from all walks of life, and including 150 congressmen, came together before the Lincoln Memorial in Washington. It was the largest demonstration in American history up to that time. And there, to the huge crowd and to the nation via TV, King gave his famous "I Have a Dream" speech. In it came those unforgettable words: "I have a dream that my four little children will one day live in a nation where they will not be judged by the color of their skin but by the content of their character. . . . I have a dream that one day this nation will rise up and live out the true meaning of its creed: We hold these truths to be self-evident, that all men are created equal. . . ."

In November 1963 the president was assassinated

Martin Luther King, Jr., waving to the immense crowd gathered near the Lincoln Memorial in Washington, D.C., where he delivered his "I Have a Dream" speech.

and Vice President Lyndon B. Johnson replaced him. The new president, despite coming from Texas, a Southern state, fought for passage of what became the Civil Rights Act of 1964. This after a yearlong debate, the longest debate on any bill in history.

FREEDOM SONGS

"Freedom songs are the soul of the movement," said Martin Luther King, Jr. Their words were not just clever slogans meant to excite campaigners. They came out of a long musical tradition in black history: the slave songs, the sorrow songs, shouts for joy, battle hymns. . . . And now for the civil rights movement. The words "Woke up this morning with my mind stayed on Freedom" were sorely needed to make them less afraid. The words, the beat, the rhythm underscored the determination that "We shall overcome, black and white together, we shall overcome someday." These songs, said King, "bound us together, gave us courage together, helped us march together." All over the South, the streets of towns and cities echoed to the music of freedom songs.

"We Shall Overcome," perhaps most closely linked to the movement, was an old Baptist hymn, "I'll Overcome Someday," combined by the folksinger Pete Seeger with a work song used by black union laborers in the 1940s, "We Will Overcome."

CHAPTER 13

Murder in Mississippi, Bloody Sunday in Selma

IT WOULD BE NEARLY A YEAR after the March on Washington before the Congress would pass the broad Civil Rights Act of 1964. It outlawed discrimination on the basis of race, color, religion, sex, age, physical handicap, or national origin; outlawed segregation in public places; created the Equal Employment Opportunity Commission to enforce the job discrimination ban; and created the Community Relations Service to mediate civil rights disputes with local officials.

Other civil rights measures had been adopted earlier, in 1957 and 1960, but ignored or poorly enforced. This landmark law was designed to expand, strengthen, and provide enforcement of civil rights.

The ban on job discrimination did not have

much immediate effect, but the provision requiring the integration of public places worked. Few places resisted the new federal law openly, though some tried to discourage black customers by discourteous service.

Earlier, while the new bill was still being debated, civil rights groups in Mississippi had been trying to move against monumental resistance. By 1963 the U.S. Commission on Civil Rights was voicing increasing alarm at the way Mississippi defied the Constitution: "Each week brings fresh evidence of the danger of a complete breakdown of law and order. Citizens have been shot, set upon by vicious dogs, and otherwise terrorized because they sought to vote. . . . Students have been fired upon, ministers have been assaulted. . . . Even children, at the brink of starvation, have been deprived of assistance by the callous and discriminatory acts of Mississippi officials administering Federal funds. All this affronts the conscience of the Nation."

That was no news to the young activists. Their Freedom Riders had already spent much time in Mississippi jails. Since 1961 a group of SNCC workers had been building a base in the town of McComb. Robert Moses was their leader. A Harvard-educated schoolteacher from Harlem, he hoped to create a model for community organization that could be followed in other places. Working closely with local black leaders, Moses helped build their confidence in their ability to continue the struggle after SNCC would leave.

It was hard going. After nearly three years of work in Mississippi, in the state with the largest black population in America, only 5 percent of voting-age blacks had registered—the lowest percentage in the nation. In a symbolic election in the fall of 1963, 80,000 disfranchised blacks had voted on a Freedom Ballot for their candidates for governor and lieutenant governor. Eighty white students had come down to help carry out the Freedom Vote campaign. The media, intrigued by how this was done, gave SNCC the kind of publicity its earlier efforts had not received. Robert Moses concluded that if even larger numbers of white college students from the North came in to help, it would protect the movement from white violence. And if it did occur, the Northern press would pay attention to it, as it rarely did to violence against Mississippi blacks.

The predominantly black Council of Federated Organizations (COFO)—an alliance of CORE, the NAACP, SCLC, and SNCC—recruited students throughout the country to come to Mississippi for the 1964 Freedom Summer Project. They would join in an all-out effort to register voters in support of the newly organized Mississippi Freedom Democratic Party (MFDP).

The aim of the new party was to provide a political

channel through which blacks and whites devoted to civil rights could organize and act. The old all-white Democratic Party, thoroughly racist since the days of Reconstruction, must be challenged to change or go down in defeat.

About 800 college students answered the call—from schools like Harvard, Swarthmore, Berkeley, Oberlin, Bryn Mawr, Mount Holyoke. . . . Three out of four were white, and half were women. Black SNCC veterans put them through an intense training program in nonviolent principles and methods on the campus of the Western College for Women in Oxford, Ohio. They were told of the hatred they faced, of the great risks—injury, perhaps death.

They were ready to face the challenge. COFO believed that the segregationist laws keeping more than 90 percent of Mississippi's eligible blacks from voting could be successfully overcome. If the worst segregationist state in the Union could be cracked, the rest of the South would follow.

Even as the volunteers arrived in Mississippi in June, they learned that three civil rights workers—Andrew Goodman, twenty, Michael Schwerner, twenty-four, and James Chaney, twenty-one—were missing. On June 21 they had been passing through the town of Philadelphia, Mississippi, on their way to investigate the burning of a nearby church. Arrested on the false charge of speeding, they were briefly jailed, and then released, at night. Driving ahead on their mission, they were followed by deputies—and then they disappeared.

A massive search for the missing men ended when a tipoff led to the discovery of three bodies buried in an earthen dam. They had been shot, and one, Chaney, the black, had been brutally beaten. Months later, several whites, including police, were implicated in the murders. But charges were dropped in state court. Then the federal government stepped in, with charges of civil rights violations. Eventually, seven were tried for conspiracy, convicted, and sent to prison.

The burned station wagon of three missing civil rights workers, found in a swampy region near Philadelphia, Mississippi, in the summer of 1964. The lynched victims were James Chaney, an African American, and Michael Schwerner and Andrew Goodman, whites.

The three men were not the first civil rights victims in Mississippi, a state that between 1882 and 1952 had 534 reported lynchings. What was different this time was that two—Goodman and Schwerner—were white. And this time neither the media nor the public ignored their deaths.

The Freedom Summer Project went on, despite the frightening murders. From mid-June to mid-September, movement people reported more than 450 incidents. There were over a thousand arrests of civil rights workers, 80 beatings, 35 shootings, 37 black church burnings, 30 bombings. The press reported every incident, exposing to the whole nation the evil of white supremacy in the Deep South.

Both the volunteers and the local people gained experience in community organizing. Among the best accomplishments were the voter registration schools, or "freedom schools." They used innovative methods to bring black children and often their parents the kind of empowering knowledge their own schools never touched. Especially was this true of African American history. Out of those summer schools came the free schools movement that took hold in Northern cities soon after. The experience of Freedom Summer led a large number of volunteers to stay on as SNCC field workers.

They helped to build the new integrated political

organization meant to challenge the legitimacy of the all-white official Democratic Party in Mississippi. That August in Atlantic City, where the Democrats held their presidential nominating convention, the sixty-eight delegates of the Mississippi Freedom Democratic Party hoped to unseat the white regulars by claiming they, the MFDP delegates, were the people who truly represented the principles of the national party, not the others. And at the same time they affirmed their support for the reelection of President Johnson.

One of the college students in the Mississippi Freedom School Project working with a black child.

Those sixty-eight were ordinary people, black and white—carpenters, maids, farmers, painters, field hands, mechanics, teachers, the young, the old—with a just cause to present.

Although many of the delegates from the Northern states supported the MFDP, the challenge failed. President Johnson feared that he could lose the entire South if the white Mississippi delegation were forced to share power with the MFDP. So he offered the MFDP two seats at the convention rather than deal with the issues they raised. The MFDP rejected what they called a back-of-the-bus offer. It was just tokenism. They would accept only the full recognition of their constitutional rights. They had played the game honestly and bravely, only to find the door slammed in their faces. Power politics, not people politics, had won this round.

That would be the last Freedom Summer. In November, when SNCC met to assess the results, many blacks argued it was time for SNCC to go it alone. They believed "if we are to proceed towards true liberation, we must cut ourselves off from white people."

About a year later, whites were officially expelled from SNCC. The black-white coalitions of the 1960s were falling apart.

Black-white unity had helped the movement to get closer to its goal of securing voting rights. But some wondered if this new turn toward "going it alone" would be the answer to another deeply troubling question: How could the basic living conditions of poor African Americans be improved? Would the ballot be enough? What about the grim facts of poor-paying jobs or no jobs at all, about rat-infested tenements and broken-down shacks, about crumbling schools with poorly trained teachers and the lowest funding, about overcrowded hospitals in urban ghettoes . . . ?

After Atlantic City, the SNCC worker Charles Sherrod said, "We are what we are—hungry, beaten, unvictorious, jobless, homeless, but thankful to have the strength to fight . . . and we refuse to compromise."

Recognition of the great contribution the movement had made to the value of peaceful, nonviolent resistance to injustice came a few months later. On December 10, 1964, Martin Luther King received the Nobel Peace Prize. Speaking in Stockholm, he said:

I accept this award today with an abiding faith in America and an audacious faith in the future of mankind. . . . I believe that wounded justice, lying prostrate on the blood-flowing streets of our nations, can be lifted from this dust of shame to reign supreme among the children of men. I have the audacity to believe that peoples everywhere can have three meals

Martin Luther King, Jr., just after receiving the Nobel Peace Prize in Oslo, Norway, on December 10, 1964. On the right is Mrs. King.

a day for their bodies, education and culture for their minds, and dignity, equality, and freedom for their spirits. . . . I still believe that we shall overcome. . . .

A month later, King arrived in Selma, Alabama, to take part in the ongoing voter registration drive that SNCC had begun a year before. The same ugly pattern of denial of voting rights flourished in Selma as it had in Albany, Birmingham, and thousands of other communities in the South.

Freedom Days were launched, to mobilize people to test and challenge the barriers to the ballot box. On February 1 a huge crowd of African Americans assembled at a church to walk together to the courthouse to register.

They were from every walk of black life in Selma—
schoolteachers, maids, housewives, beauticians, under-
takers, men, women, children. Faceless people to out-
siders, nameless, unknown. But they were *the movement*.

These were dramatic highlights in the movement's
history. But all across the South, there were protests every
day. "People silently walked a picket line for hours on
end," said John Lewis, "or sang freedom songs from dawn

Black Atlantans picket downtown department stores for discriminating against shoppers.

to dusk, or simply stood on line at a door they knew would not be opened, hour after hour, day after day. The patience and persistence it took to endure those countless hours of weary boredom in stifling heat or bone-chilling cold, in driving rain and wet, slushy snow is as admirable as the bravery it took to face the billy clubs of those deputies."

About 800 were arrested on February 1. Among them were 500 girls and boys from Selma's schools, some carrying crayoned protest signs. And King too was jailed.

Five days later, King was released. He went right to Washington, where the Administration promised him it would present Congress with a voting rights bill to enforce black registration of qualified voters. But not right now. Maybe next year? The year after?

Meanwhile, resistance by Selma's whites went on. While hundreds of black citizens attempted to register, only fifty-seven were allowed into the registrar's office, where they were given a literacy test. And none of those received notice of successful registration. "The test is so ridiculous," said King to the press, "that even Chief Justice Warren might fail to answer some questions." While America had declared war against totalitarianism around the world, he said, here blacks are beaten by the sheriff and his deputies and people have been fired from their jobs. Why? Because they tried to exercise their simple right to vote. It is time that the president, the Congress, and the courts declare war against oppression and totalitarianism right here at home.

Some congressmen got the idea, and fifteen of them flew in to see for themselves what was going on in Selma. Sheriff Jim Clark obliged them by arresting some 500 more marchers. And soon after, he hurled Selma into the headlines again by arresting 160 teenagers and herding them on a forced run of some two miles out into the countryside, with his deputies using clubs and cattle prods to keep the youngsters moving. Several were beaten on the way. One nine-year-old was forced to run the distance barefoot.

A fifty-four-mile freedom march from Selma to the state capitol at Montgomery was planned for March 7. The movement knew from experience that such non-violent direct-action campaigns might meet with violence. "I can't promise you that you won't get beaten," King told the people in Selma the night before. King himself would not be there, for he felt he could not miss still another Sunday in his own pulpit in Atlanta.

When Governor Wallace issued a ban on the march, the movement leaders expected state troopers would be there to arrest the demonstrators. But no one imagined what the governor actually had planned. As the marchers streamed across the Pettus Bridge onto Highway 80, they were halted in front by a line of battle-ready state troopers. Then, from behind, with no warning, the sheriff's deputies and city police, all armed and some on horseback, attacked them with tear gas, clubs, whips, and electric cattle prods. The screaming, bleeding marchers fled for their lives, the lawmen chasing them back into the city, clubbing them as they ran nearly a mile. More than ninety were seriously hurt—fractured skulls, wrists, arms, legs, jaws, teeth.

That scene at the Pettus Bridge was witnessed by millions that evening on the national television news. It was like a nightmare. Could this be real? people asked. Could men sworn to uphold law and order make this murderous assault upon defenseless American citizens peacefully marching for a just cause?

The whole country—the whole world!—saw what had happened on Bloody Sunday in Selma. And the next day people from all over America began arriving to help the cause of civil rights. In the two days following Bloody Sunday, there were demonstrations in more than eighty cities protesting the violence and calling for passage of a voting rights act.

On March 9 there was another march, led by King. This time a federal judge issued an injunction forbidding it. Despite that order, the demonstrators, joined by hundreds of ministers and others who had come to Selma to make witness, marched until they faced the troopers in a

Alabama state troopers block the highway as civil rights demonstrators, black and white, come over the Pettus Bridge on March 9, 1965.

solid line blocking Highway 80. Then they turned around. They felt they had made their point. They had revealed again the constant threat of violence.

That night, a white Unitarian minister from Boston, the Rev. James Reeb, was murdered by whites as he walked past a Selma café. They shouted, "Nigger lover!" as they beat him to death with iron bars.

This climax to the mad violence infuriated President Johnson. On March 15 he spoke to a joint session of Congress. He made the strongest commitment to full civil rights that any president has ever made:

It is not just Negroes, but really it is all of us who must overcome the crippling legacy of bigotry and injustice. . . . And we shall overcome.

So a third march from Selma to Montgomery began, on March 21. This time it was a triumphal celebration. A safe passage was guaranteed by President Johnson, who had called the Alabama National Guard into federal service. Blacks and whites, Protestants, Catholics, and Jews joined together on the route to the state capitol. They reached Montgomery on March 25, 30,000 nonviolent crusaders from every county in Alabama and almost every state in the Union.

Speaking on the grounds of the capitol, King asked again and again, "How long?" and each time he answered, "Not long." Had they reached the Promised Land?

The night after King's moving speech, Mrs. Viola Liuzzo, a white civil rights activist from Detroit, was driving her car back to Montgomery after carrying some marchers back to Selma when Klan night riders shot her to death on a lonely stretch of highway.

But Selma, and what the nation had learned from it, brought about the Voting Rights Act of 1965. For the first time, the new law took the registration of blacks out of the hands of state registrars in regions of recorded discrimination and placed the power of the federal government behind the right to vote. It produced a greater change in American politics than any single piece of legislation had ever done.

Signed into law on August 6, 1965, the act led quickly to the elections of a number of black public officials. Where in 1964 there had been only sixteen black state legislators in the South, by 1966 there were thirty-seven, and by 1970 the number had doubled again to seventy-three. Southern voters sent two blacks to Congress in 1972 and a third in 1974. They were the first to enter Congress from the South in more than seventy years. By 1999, the century's end, the Black Caucus in Congress numbered thirty-nine members of the House of Representatives.

Selma, Selma, Selma . . . That protest movement was crucial in bringing about the Voting Rights Act. It was the result of what African Americans themselves had so skillfully done to build a national consensus in favor of the bill.

Now blacks would have some say, much more say, in how local and state and federal government operated. But it did not create heaven on earth. There were limits to what has happened since then. Little occurred to change the fact of black poverty or to wipe out the black ghetto. By focusing on ballots for blacks in the South, it is easy to forget the North. Didn't black people there have the right to vote long before Selma? But what had that done to lift black people out of poverty? To provide jobs at decent wages? To replace slum housing?

If the civil rights movement and the American public generally were blind to that reality, something happened in the summer of 1965 to open everyone's eyes.

CHAPTER 14

Where Now?

FOR IN THAT SUMMER OF 1965, within days after the Voting Rights Act finally became law, the fires of Watts broke out. For six days, there was terrible rioting in that black section of Los Angeles. It was the explosion that for years some had sensed would happen. By the time the fires died down, 34 people were dead, over 800 were injured, and 3,000 had been arrested. Nor was the violence confined to the West Coast. Riots broke out in New York, Cleveland, Chicago, South Bend, Jacksonville . . .

In 1967 riots erupted again, this time in 164 cities, with 82 dead, 3,400 injured, and 4,000 arrested. A Commission on Civil Disorders appointed by President Johnson warned that "Our nation is moving toward two societies, one black, one white—separate and unequal." White

A National Guard Jeep patrols the burned-out Watts section of Los Angeles in the summer of 1965, just after one of the worst riots in the nation's history.

violence was the root cause of the riots, it concluded, urging immediate public and private action to rebuild the urban ghettoes. It was a bleak picture of the responsibilities of white America for those continuing disasters.

Should the riots have been a surprise? No, says black historian Vincent Harding. "Anyone who looked at the conditions of the black communities, anyone who recognized the all-too-American commitment to violent solutions then being acted out in Vietnam, anyone who felt the increasing white resistance to deep probes into the structural problems of the nation—anyone with such insights knew that something like Watts was coming."

But do riots do any good? John Lewis, chairman of

SNCC at the time, and later a congressman from Georgia, said that rioting on this scale "frightened me. Rioting is not a movement. It is not an act of civil disobedience. I think it is a mistake for people to consider disorganized action, mayhem, and attacks on other people and property as an extension of any kind of movement. It is not. It is simply an explosion of emotion. That's all. There is nothing constructive about it. It is only *de*structive."

Yet he continued, "Where lack of jobs, intolerable housing, police brutality, and other frustrating conditions exist, it is possible that violence and massive street demonstrations may develop."

True, blacks now had the right to vote, and they could eat at lunch counters or any ritzier place. That is, if they had the money to pay for it. And millions didn't. To fight against segregation, one effect of racism, was one thing. But to combat racism, the virus embedded deep in American society and in all its institutions, that was something else.

What to do about it was a question that was tearing at the vitals of the movement. By this time leaders of the movement as well as increasing numbers of the general population saw the war in Vietnam as cruel, unjust, and wasteful. Young blacks were being sent to Asia to protect the rights of the people of South Vietnam while the rights of black people at home were being violated daily.

Stokely Carmichael, SNCC leader, distributes a leaflet outside the Atlanta, Georgia, military induction center in 1967. At right is a copy of the leaflet, which urges blacks not to support the war in Vietnam.

Although blacks were but 10 percent of the American population, by the end of 1965 about 60 percent of the American troops were black. And one out of every four of the soldiers dying in battle was black.

Black GIs were being asked to kill strangers in Vietnam while their own family and friends were being killed at home in Mississippi or Georgia or Alabama. Everyone would remember what Muhammad Ali, the world heavyweight boxing champion, said when as a conscientious objector he refused service in that war: "No Viet Cong ever called me nigger!"

And beyond this issue was what the war was doing to the whole of America. President Johnson had launched a War on Poverty. The Economic Opportunity Act of 1964 was only an experiment, and the program eventually faded out. The passage of Medicare, health insurance for the elderly, was an advance upon FDR's Social Security legislation. In 1965 support was given to education legislation that proved of considerable help to schools everywhere.

But soon the country's resources were being drained away to pay for the troops and bullets and bombs and planes and ships thrown into battle halfway around the world. Guns or butter? Guns won out. Between 1946 and 1967, the federal government spent $904 billion on military power against $96 billion on social needs such as education, health, and welfare.

Within the military, although segregation had been forbidden, discrimination continued. During the Vietnam

After fighting in a ten-day mission in Vietnam, troops stand in a chow line serving Christmas turkey on December 25, 1966.

War, there were few black officers. In 1967 there were only two black generals among 1,346 generals and admirals—one each in the army and air force. The marines had no black colonels. Only two battalion commanders out of 380 on the battlefield were black.

The Civil Disorders Commission, chaired by Governor Otto Kerner of Illinois, made many proposals for improving living and working conditions for blacks. But neither President Johnson nor President Nixon endorsed them. Little was done beyond some small gestures to carry out the Kerner recommendations. White "law and order" candidates for public office successfully preyed on public fear of crime and disorder and continue to do so. They called for greater armed control of the ghettoes, for more police, more weapons, stiffer penalties, and more prisons.

Where should the movement go? In what direction? It could be justly proud of its achievements of the last decade. It had won voting rights for blacks in the South, yes. But everywhere there were still poor, sick, ill-educated blacks—and whites. This was a society that produced great wealth for a small minority while it left tens of millions in misery.

The feeble response to the "Kerner Report" was proof to King and the SCLC that government would not move to solve a problem involving race unless it was confronted head-on. King believed they had to go to Washington, demand to be heard, and stay there until America listened, and acted.

The program laid out was an economic bill of rights—to guarantee housing integration, provide jobs, and establish a guaranteed annual income for all. The method: to mobilize thousands of poor people to march into the nation's capital and create "massive dislocations" until their demands were met. It would be a campaign for jobs and income, crucial not only to black people but to poor people of whatever color.

In March 1968 King traveled the country, making many speeches to build support for the Poor People's Campaign. From Los Angeles he flew into Memphis, where 1,300 sanitation workers, public employees, were on strike. "One day our society will come to respect the sanitation worker if it is to survive," he said, "for the person who picks up our garbage is, in the final analysis, as significant as the physician, for if he doesn't do his job, diseases are rampant. All labor has dignity." He warned that "if America does not use her vast resources of wealth to end poverty and make it possible for all God's children to have the basic necessities of life, it will go to hell."

In Memphis, he made what would be his final speech, in which he seemed to foretell his own imminent death. And the next day, April 4, 1968, standing on a

Soldiers stand amid the rubble of a burned-out building in downtown Washington on April 6, 1968. Riots that lasted days broke out in many cities after the assassination of Martin Luther King, Jr., on April 4, 1968.

motel balcony before dinner, he was shot to death. The appalling news of his murder triggered riots in more than 100 cities.

A white man was charged with the crime, convicted, and sent to prison. Many years later, the King family questioned his guilt and alleged King was the victim of a broad conspiracy.

With King's death, the civil rights movement, already torn by dissent within it, lost its unity of purpose. The Poor People's Campaign, led now by the Rev. Ralph Abernathy, King's successor as head of the SCLC, fizzled out. In May it drew not thousands but only several hundred demonstrators of all races to Washington. They built a tent-and-plywood Resurrection City. It suffered from bad weather, a small predatory group of criminals, and ethnic conflicts. And the increasing conservatism of the Johnson Administration, as well as the Congress, provided no support. Before June ended, the campaigners had given up and were gone.

It was the end of the main drive of the civil rights movement. In 1968 Richard Nixon was elected president. His victory owed much to the white South and to racist emotions in the North. Yet surprisingly, in spite of many steps backward, his Administration did establish some affirmative action procedures. Their aim was to compensate minorities and women for past discrimination in jobs and education by giving them certain advantages to offset the old, deep-rooted handicaps. For the next ten years, blacks and women moved closer to statistical parity in the colleges and in professional schools, in jobs and in income.

When Nixon left the White House in 1973, resigning in disgrace after Watergate, he was followed in turn by Gerald Ford, Jimmy Carter, Ronald Reagan, George Bush, and Bill Clinton. Three Republicans and two Democrats. None of them did much to improve conditions for the disinherited. They and the majority in Congress favored affirmative action, yes, but only through tax policies favoring the wealthy and the powerful. The others—they could look after themselves. (The rich were richer than ever. The top 10 percent of the population in the late 1990s had wealth equal to the bottom 90 percent.) About one in every four children lived in poverty.

Politicians generally continued to ignore the great numbers of blacks who could not climb the rungs on the ladder of social mobility. As the millennium year 2000 came on, these were the harsh facts: In jobs, only 52 percent of black men had full-time, year-round work. In public education, nearly 70 percent of black students were attending schools with predominantly minority enrollment. "Racial progress," said Nicolaus Mills, a veteran of the civil rights movement, "has slowed down to a crawl."

What about the African Americans who "made it"? Those who have reached into the middle class? An extensive study of the black middle-class experience, made in the 1990s by two sociologists, Joe R. Feagin and Melvin P. Sikes, had this to report on what it is like to be a black person in white America today:

Clearly, no amount of hard work and achievement, no amount of money, resources, and success, can protect black people from the persisting ravages of white racism in their everyday lives. . . . Racial stereotyping,

prejudice, and hostility still operate indiscriminately,
despite the actual identities and achievements of the
black individuals discriminated against. . . .

The classic American creed promises the
inalienable rights of "Life, Liberty, and the Pursuit
of Happiness" today for all citizens of this democratic
nation. Yet after several centuries of struggle these
rights are not even close to being secured for all black
Americans, including middle-class black Americans.
Perhaps the greatest tragedy in our findings of
widespread racism is that they reveal the
much-celebrated American creed to be little more
than hollow words.

Nevertheless, we can't forget that the civil rights movement of the 1950s and 1960s made a remarkable leap forward. Think of how much worse things would be if there had not been those victories. But the movement lost its steam more than thirty years ago. Many blacks, and many whites too, turned cynical. They dropped out of the democratic process. They didn't vote.

Is it right to blame politicians for everything wrong? Does it do ourselves or America any good to just quit? The media rarely report it, but millions of Americans have begun to realize that democracy is not what we have: IT IS WHAT WE DO.

Looking ahead to what might make a difference, the Harvard professor William Julius Wilson has made a proposal. He calls for a national multiracial coalition to press for political change. Political power, he points out, is concentrated among the best-off members of society. Government policies affecting economic life benefit these white elites while leaving ordinary people to fall farther behind.

What could reverse the trends of rising inequality and ease the burdens of the disadvantaged? Nothing, so long as middle- and lower-class groups are fragmented along racial lines. If Americans continue to stress racial differences rather than what people have in common, it will be hard to see the need for helping one another across racial lines.

Wilson wasn't calling for the formation of a new political party. He sees a coalition as officially nonpartisan. Its aim would be to put pressure, including voting pressure, on both Democratic and Republican leaders to embrace policies that reflect the interests of ordinary families. When such a coalition grows strong enough, both parties are likely to listen to its demands.

As for who would make up such a coalition, Wilson says its foundation would be "organizations committed to fighting social inequality, including grassroots community organizations, civil rights groups, women's rights groups, labor unions, and religious organizations. All broadly representative of the various racial and ethnic groups, and all organized in interconnected local, regional, and national networks."

When you think of the great numbers of people already members of, and active in, these many groups, you can see how a coalition would speak for millions. It wouldn't be easy to bring so many groups together. The media constantly highlight those racial factors that divide Americans. Those factors are real, but the increasing attention given to them conceals the basic truth that blacks, whites, Latinos, Asians, and Native Americans "share many concerns and have important values and aspirations in common." A multiracial coalition would bring together all groups who are struggling to make a decent living, not just poor minorities.

When people believe they need each other, says Wilson, history shows that they give up their initial prejudices and stereotypes and join programs that encourage mutual interaction and cooperation.

Lord knows there is bad news aplenty to undermine hope—war, discrimination, prejudice, poverty, hunger, crime, failing schools. But millions of people have not given up. They protest, make demands, and above all, they organize at local and regional levels. They focus on specific, realizable campaigns through ground-level initiatives that can meet with success.

When we come together, we can solve problems.

Every one of us is capable of helping to shape the direction of schools, the workplace, the community—and government. Just as the civil rights movement reshaped the institutions of local, state, and federal government in its heyday. History has shown that was a great achievement, but history doesn't stand still. More, much more, has yet to be done, and it is up to Americans to pitch in and do it.

> ## BLACK POWER
> No one reading the press or watching TV in the last half of the 1960s was unaware of "Black Power." The term gained popularity when Stokely Carmichael, a leader of SNCC, used it in a series of speeches. As a political idea, Black Power had its roots in a tradition of black nationalism going back to the nineteenth century. Such figures as Marcus Garvey and, later, Malcolm X believed that blacks should work for self-determination rather than integration, and that blacks had the right to retaliate when attacked violently.
>
> More a slogan than a program, Black Power came out of deep disappointment over the slow and limited gains of the movement, and out

of bitterness over violent white opposition to the most minimal black gains.

Many ideas were associated with the slogan: pride in racial identity, the need to study black history, the desirability of blacks controlling their own institutions. But there were many clashes, sometimes deadly, between users of the slogan. It all showed how diverse black political life had become.

Militant young blacks decided they had turned their cheek too often. And what had they to show for it? Full desegregation now appeared to be an illusion. Let's battle for self-determination instead, they said, use our right of self-defense, strike back when we are struck. Several black groups picked up on Black Power and developed their own variations on it. Rather than pursue extreme separation, others attracted to Black Power strove to increase the number of black-owned businesses and black officeholders.

But to most whites Black Power was a scary slogan. Did it mean violence would enter the peaceful and affluent suburbs? "To that extent," wrote the historians William Chafe and Harvard Sitkoff, "Black Power helped to polarize the races, sanction the cult of violence, fuel the white backlash, and destroy the civil rights movement. Yet it also generated valuable changes. It galvanized many whom the movement had never mobilized. It spawned a vast array of new community organizations. It spurred self-reliance. It focused attention on the needs of the lower classes. It forced the nation to contemplate the plight of powerlessness. Fundamentally, Black Power made blacks proud to be black, a psychological precondition for equality."

Teenagers and children give the Black Panther salute to Black Power on the steps of their Liberation School in the Fillmore district of San Francisco in 1969.

A Calendar of
Civil Rights History
1940–1968

This chronology begins in 1940, on the eve of America's entry into World War II, and concludes in 1968, when the period known as the civil rights movement came to an end.

1940   12,865,518 blacks in United States, 9.8 percent of population. Benjamin O. Davis appointed brigadier general, first black to become general in U.S. armed forces.

1941   First Army Air Corps squadron for black cadets formed by War Department at Tuskegee, Alabama. New York bus companies agree to hire black drivers and mechanics. March on Washington movement wins from President Roosevelt his Executive Order 8802, forbidding racial and

A Maryland restaurant in 1948 with a "White Only" sign over the front entrance directing "Colored" to the back door.

religious discrimination in war plants, government training programs, and government industries. Fair Employment Practices Commission is appointed to carry out order. Supreme Court rules separate facilities on railroads must be equal.

1942 Race riot in Detroit, one of several racial incidents to occur during war. U.S. Navy gives first commission to a black, Harvard medical student Bernard W. Robinson. Congress of Racial Equality organized in Chicago and stages first sit-in in local restaurant. Hugh Mulzac is first black captain to command a U.S. merchant ship, the *Booker T. Washington*.

1943 Race riots in Mobile, Beaumont (Texas), Detroit, Harlem.

1944 Supreme Court rules blacks cannot be denied right to vote in a primary election (*Smith* v. *Allwright*). Adam Clayton Powell of New York is first black congressman to be elected in the East.

1945 New York is first state to adopt an FEPC law. World War II ends with 1,154,720 blacks having served in the armed forces.

1946 Race riots in Tennessee, Alabama, and Philadelphia. Supreme Court bans segregation in interstate bus travel. President Truman issues executive order establishing Commission on Civil Rights.

1947 First Freedom Rider group sent by CORE on Southern tour. "To Secure These Rights," report attacking racial injustice in the United States, is issued by President's Commission on Civil Rights. NAACP appeals to the United Nations on same issue.

The young Roy Wilkins, leader of the NAACP.

1948   Supreme Court rules that a state must provide legal education for blacks at the same time it provides it for whites, and that federal and state courts may not enforce restrictive covenants in housing. President Truman issues executive order requiring equality of treatment and opportunity in the armed forces.

1949   William H. Hastie is nominated for U.S. Circuit Court of Appeals. William L. Dawson chosen chairman of House Expenditures Committee, is first black to head standing committee of Congress. Wesley A. Brown is first black graduated from Annapolis Naval Academy.

1950   15,042,286 blacks in United States, 10 percent of population. Supreme Court rules that equality in education involves more than physical facilities, rules that students admitted to a school cannot be segregated, and bans Jim Crow in railroad dining cars.

1951   Racial segregation is ruled illegal in restaurants of Washington, D.C., and racial discrimination is prohibited in New York's city-assisted housing projects. The first black student is admitted to the University of North Carolina. An NAACP official in Florida, Harry T. Moore, is killed when his home is wrecked by a bomb.

1952   This is the first year since 1881 for which the Tuskegee Institute record shows no lynchings in the United States.

1953   Whites begin protracted series of riots to protest against blacks moving into Chicago's Trumbull Park housing project. Rufus Clement elected to Atlanta Board of Education and Hulan Jack to borough presidency of Manhattan. President Eisenhower sets up Government Contract Compliance Committee to police ban on discrimination in government contracts.

1954   Supreme Court rules that racial segregation in public schools is unconstitutional. School integration begins in the capital and in Baltimore. Black units are abolished in armed forces. Charles C. Diggs, Jr., is elected Michigan's first black congressman. Benjamin O. Davis, Jr., appointed first black general in Air Force.

1955   Supreme Court orders school integration "with all deliberate speed" and bans segregation in public recreation facilities. Segregation in buses, waiting rooms, and railroad coaches in interstate travel is banned by the Interstate Commerce Commission. Emmet Till, fourteen, is kidnapped and lynched in Mississippi. A bus boycott begins in Montgomery, Alabama, under the leadership of the Rev. Martin Luther King, Jr.

1956 Autherine J. Lucy admitted to University of Alabama but expelled twenty-six days later. Supreme Court upholds ban on segregation in intrastate bus travel. Bus boycotts in Birmingham and Tallahassee. National Guard used to quell mobs trying to prevent school integration in Clinton, Tennessee, and Sturgis, Kentucky. Louisville integrates its public schools.

A high school student in Clinton, Tennessee, in 1956 protests a federal court decision ordering the desegregation of his school.

1957 Southern Christian Leadership Conference organized in New Orleans; Rev. Martin Luther King, Jr., elected president. First Civil Rights Act since 1875 passed by Congress. Federal troops ordered to Little Rock to ensure that nine black children enter Central High School. Tuskegee blacks boycott merchants to protest gerrymander depriving blacks of municipal vote. New York City's Fair Housing Practices Law is first municipal measure against racial and religious discrimination in housing.

Civil rights leaders join hands at a Freedom Pilgrimage Rally in Washington, D.C., in May 1957. From left: Roy Wilkins of the NAACP, the Rev. Martin Luther King, Jr., and A. Philip Randolph, head of the Brotherhood of Sleeping Car Porters.

1958   Sit-ins used to desegregate Oklahoma City lunch counters. Philadelphia elects Robert N. C. Nix to Congress.

1959   To prevent school integration, Prince Edward County in Virginia closes public school system. Mack Parker lynched in Poplarville, Mississippi.

1960   18,871,831 blacks in United States, 10.5 percent of population. Students of North Carolina Agricultural and Technical College begin sit-in movement at five-and-ten store in Greensboro, North Carolina. Tactic swiftly adopted by students in fifteen cities in five Southern states. First Southern city to integrate lunch counters is San Antonio. National chain stores follow in over 100 cities. Thousands of students arrested

Demonstrators are loaded into a police van in Albany, Georgia, in 1962 after trying to integrate local eating places.

in demonstrations, some suspended by colleges. Student Nonviolent Coordinating Committee organized at Shaw University. Congress passes Civil Rights Act of 1960. Large demonstrations against Jim Crow in Atlanta.

1961 Adam Clayton Powell becomes chairman of House Education and Labor Committee. Robert C. Weaver made chief of Housing and Home Finance Agency, highest federal appointment thus far for a black. Otis M. Smith appointed to Michigan Supreme Court. Freedom Riders on bus trip through South attacked, bombed, burned, arrested in Alabama and Mississippi. ICC prohibits segregation on buses and in terminal facilities. President Kennedy appoints Thurgood Marshall to U.S. Circuit Court of Appeals. Militant Albany Movement uses mass marches on City Hall to protest segregation and discrimination in that Georgia city. Board of Education of New Rochelle, New York, ordered by judge to integrate schools.

1962 James H. Meredith, escorted by federal marshals, registered at University of Mississippi after 1,200 federal soldiers restore order on rioting campus. Two are killed and over 100 wounded in violence touched off at Governor

James H. Meredith, an army veteran, escorted by a U.S. marshal to classes at the University of Mississippi in 1962.

Ross Barnett's defiance of federal court order to admit Meredith. SNCC works on voter registration in South, especially in Mississippi. Pressure applied against de facto segregation in Northern school systems. President Kennedy issues order against racial and religious discrimination in federally financed housing.

1963   Centennial of Emancipation Proclamation is celebrated by intensified campaigns for civil rights. Two black students enrolled at University of Alabama under escort of federal troops. Medgar Evers, NAACP leader in Mississippi, murdered in front of his home. Discrimination in building trades unions protested by mass demonstrations at Harlem building sites. A quarter of a million blacks and whites take part in March on Washington for civil rights. Four black children killed when Birmingham church is bombed. Some 225,000 students boycott Chicago public schools for one day to protest de facto segregation.

Malcolm X addressing a civil rights rally in Harlem in 1963.

1964   Almost a million students boycott New York City public schools on one day and another quarter million students on a later day. Civil Rights Act with public accommodation and fair employment sections passed by Congress and signed by President Lyndon B. Johnson on July 3 after Senate uses cloture to stop a Southern filibuster. Race riots erupt in New York City, Rochester, Jersey City, Chicago, Philadelphia. Civil rights organizations undertake Mississippi Freedom Project during summer, opening freedom schools and community centers and aiding blacks to register to vote. Three young civil rights workers engaged in project are murdered by segregationists near Philadelphia, Mississippi. Freedom Democratic Party, organized in Mississippi, nominates three blacks for Congress, the first since Reconstruction. Dr. Martin Luther King, Jr., awarded the Nobel Prize for Peace, viewing it as recognition of nonviolence precept.

1965   Black voter registration drive launched in Selma, Alabama, by SCLC and SNCC. When violence is used against demonstrators on Pettus Bridge, a Selma-to-Montgomery march is held to dramatize black voting rights. 3,200 blacks and whites from all over the nation go on march, protected by 4,000 troops. March ends with rally of 30,000 in front of the capitol in Montgomery. President Johnson signs the 1965 Voting Rights Act on August 6. Federal examiners begin to register blacks under the act, the first use of federal registrars since Reconstruction. The new act provides for suspension of literacy tests and for federal registration of blacks in states and subdivisions where less than 50 percent of the

Boys take part in a civil rights march in the 1960s.

177

voting-age population were registered or enrolled in November 1964. The areas covered by the law include two million unregistered blacks. Riots occur in the Watts area of Los Angeles and in Chicago. Blacks end a three-month boycott of white merchants in Natchez after the city government and business leaders agree to demands for a voice in city affairs.

1966   Robert C. Weaver, appointed Secretary of Housing and Urban Development, becomes first black Cabinet member. Constance Baker Motley is first black woman appointed a federal judge. U.S. Supreme Court rules Virginia poll tax unconstitutional, thereby ending tax in three other Southern states. Black group occupies deactivated U.S. Air Force base in Greenville, Mississippi, protesting lack of jobs and land. James Meredith begins 200-mile march from Memphis to Jackson to bolster voting registration and is shot in the back from ambush. Other civil rights leaders join march, which concludes with rally of 15,000 before state capitol at Jackson. In Mississippi primaries, 35,000 blacks vote, largest number in state in twentieth century. Black Power slogan raised by SNCC leader Stokely Carmichael during Mississippi march

U.S. athletes Tommie Smith (center) and John Carlos, star runners, raise their arms skyward in protest against racism when they receive medals at the Olympics in Mexico City in 1968.

becomes national issue. The Black Power movement, rejecting the nonviolent, integrationist, coalition-building approach of traditional civil rights groups, advocates black control of black organizations—black self-determination. Rev. Martin Luther King, Jr., opens assault by SCLC on slum conditions in Chicago. Riots occur in several urban ghettoes, especially Chicago and Cleveland.

1967 Carl Stokes elected mayor of Cleveland, Ohio, the first black mayor of a major U.S. city. Others included: Richard Hatcher (Gary, Indiana, 1967); Kenneth A. Gibson (Newark, New Jersey, 1970); Thomas Bradley (Los Angeles, California, 1973); Maynard Jackson (Atlanta, Georgia, 1973).

1968 Assassination of Martin Luther King, Jr., in Memphis, Tennessee. SCLC leadership assumed by Rev. Ralph Abernathy. Poor People's March on Washington led by Rev. Ralph Abernathy. Presidential election: 51.4 percent of registered nonwhites voted compared with 44 percent in 1964. Registration of voting-age black population in 11 Southern states rose from 1,463,000 (1960) to 3,449,000 (1971), or from a total of 29.1 percent (1960) to 58.6 percent (1971).

A farm wagon drawn by two Georgia mules—symbolizing his identification with the poor—draws the coffin of the Rev. Martin Luther King, Jr., through Atlanta on April 9, 1968. Fifty thousand people, black and white, follow the funeral cortege.

Bibliography

Abraham, Henry J., and Barbara A. Perry. *Freedom and the Court: Civil Rights and Liberties in the U.S.* New York: Oxford, 1998.

Branch, Taylor. *Parting the Waters.* New York: Simon & Schuster, 1989.

———. *Pillar of Fire: America in the King Years, 1963–1965.* New York: Simon & Schuster, 1999.

Caplan, Marvin. *Farther Along: A Civil Rights Memoir.* Baton Rouge, La.: Louisiana State University, 1999.

Carson, Clayborne, ed. *The Autobiography of Martin Luther King, Jr.* New York: Warner, 1998.

———, David J. Garrow, Gerald Gill, Vincent Harding, Darlene Clark Hine, eds. *The Eyes on the Prize Civil Rights Reader.* New York: Penguin, 1991.

Colbert, David, ed. *Eyewitness to America.* New York: Vintage, 1998.

Cooney, Robert, and Helen Michalkowski, eds. *The Power of the People: Active Nonviolence in the U.S.* Culver City, Cal.: Peace Press, 1977.

Davis, Townsend. *Weary Feet, Rested Souls: A Guided History of the Civil Rights Movement*. New York: Norton, 1998.

DeSantis, Christopher, ed. *Langston Hughes and the Chicago Defender*. Urbana, Ill.: U. of Illinois, 1995.

Feagin, Joe R., and Melvin P. Sikes. *Living with Racism: The Black Middle-Class Experience*. Boston: Beacon, 1994.

Halberstam, David. *The Children*. New York: Random House, 1998.

Hale, Grace Elizabeth. *Making Whiteness: The Culture of Segregation in the South, 1890–1940*. New York: Pantheon, 1998.

Higham, John, ed. *Civil Rights and Social Wrongs: Black-White Relations Since World War II*. University Park, Pa.: Penn State University, 1997.

Hodgson, Godfrey. *America in Our Times*. New York: Vintage, 1976.

Katz, William Loren, ed. *Eyewitness: A Living Documentary of the African American Contribution to American History*. New York: Touchstone, 1995.

Levy, Peter B. *The Civil Rights Movement*. Westport, Conn.: Greenwood, 1998.

Lewis, John, with Michael D'Orso. *Walking with the Wind: A Memoir of the Movement*. New York: Simon & Schuster, 1998.

Litwack, Leon F. *Trouble in Mind: Black Southerners in the Age of Jim Crow*. New York: Knopf, 1998.

Mann, Coramae Richey. *Unequal Justice: A Question of Color*. Bloomington, Ind.: Indiana University, 1993.

Meltzer, Milton. *The Black Americans: A History in Their Own Words*. New York: HarperCollins, 1984.

Mills, Nicolaus. "Mississippi Freedom Summer, Thirty-five Years Later." *Dissent,* Summer 1999, pp. 101–103.

Miroff, Bruce. *Icons of Democracy*. New York: Basic, 1993.

Orfield, Gary, and Holly Lebowitz, eds. *Civil Rights in a New Era: Race and Justice in a Changing America*. New York: The Century Foundation, 1999.

Rhea, Joseph Tilden. *Race Pride and the American Identity*. Cambridge, Mass.: Harvard, 1997.

Shipler, David K. *A Country of Strangers: Blacks and Whites in America*. New York: Vintage, 1999.

Sitkoff, Harvard. *The Struggle for Black Equality: 1954–1992*. New York: Hill & Wang, 1993.

Unger, Irwin, and Debi Unger, eds. *The Times Were a-Changin': The Sixties Reader*. New York: Three Rivers, 1998.

Williams, Juan. *Thurgood Marshall: American Revolutionary*. New York: Times Books, 1998.

Wilson, William Julius. *The Bridge Over the Racial Divide: Rising Inequality and Coalition Politics*. Berkeley, Cal.: University of California, 1999.

Zinn, Howard. *Declarations of Independence*. New York: HarperCollins, 1990.

Photo Credits

Photos courtesy of:

AP/Wide World Photos (pp. 82, 90, 103, 112, 122, 127, 135, 141, 152, 171, 172, 174, 179).

Bettmann/CORBIS (pp. ii, x, 8, 10, 15, 17, 21, 24, 27, 30, 33, 36, 39, 41, 44, 47, 49, 52, 55, 57, 61, 63, 65, 75, 76, 77, 81, 84, 99, 102, 104, 106, 107, 109, 110, 116, 119, 129, 137, 140, 145, 150, 153, 156, 164, 166, 170, 175, 177, 181).

Hoover Institution Archives (p. 69).

Carl Iwasaki/TimePix (p. 73).

Jack Moebes/CORBIS (p. 6).

Charles Moore/Black Star (pp. 96, 125).

Charles Phillips/TimePix (p. 167).

Schomburg Center for Research in Black Culture (p. 53).

Flip Schulke/Black Star (p. 123).

Howard Sochurek/TimePix (p. 2).

Grey Villet/TimePix (p. 86).

Hank Walker/TimePix (p. 71).

Index

About the Author

MILTON MELTZER has published nearly 100 books for young people and adults in the fields of history, biography, and social issues and has also dealt with such diverse topics as the horse, gold, the potato, memory, and names. In 2001, Meltzer was awarded the prestigious Laura Ingalls Wilder Medal, for an author or illustrator whose books have made a substantial and lasting contribution to literature for children.

Among the many honors for Meltzer's books are five nominations for the National Book Award, as well as the Christopher, Jane Addams, Carter G. Woodson, Jefferson Cup, Washington Book Guild, Olive Branch, Regina, and Golden Kite awards. Many of his books have been chosen for the honor lists of the American Library Association, the National Council of Teachers of English, and the National Council for the Social Studies, as well as for the *New York Times* Best Books of the Year list.

Meltzer and his wife, Hildy, live in New York City. They have two daughters, Jane and Amy, and two grandsons, Benjamin and Zachary. Mr. Meltzer is a member of the Authors Guild, American PEN, and the Organization of American Historians.

LANDMARK BOOKS

*Find out about important people, places, and events
with Landmark Books. Written by
the finest writers of nonfiction for young readers,
Landmark Books show us where we've been
and where we're going.*